About the Cover Art
Gratitude to Heather Tolbert for granting us permission to use her artwork *Melanin Pride/Unity* on our cover. See the "About the Cover Artist" section for more information on her life and work. You can follow her at FromTheAshes05 on Facebook, SnapChat, Instagram, and Twitter.

FROM THE ASHES

RESIPISCENCE 2019

A Lenten Devotional for Dismantling White Supremacy

Edited by
Vahisha Hasan and **Nichola Torbett**

TABLE of CONTENTS

FORWARD

Memorable are the moments that forever impact and change the trajectory of one's life. For me, one of those moments came in a tentative asking of a question from the soft voice of the fierce Nichola Torbett: "I'm considering producing a Lenten devotional centered on dismantling white supremacy. Anyone want to work on that with me?" I could barely contain my "Yes! Me!"

This exchange was on a Zoom conference call with SURJ Faith, a national subgroup of Showing Up For Racial Justice (SURJ) in late 2017 and is basically the last time I slept. It's also the last time I felt disconnected in navigating the burden of white supremacy in faith settings and the global systems that run on its oppression. From her original idea of a duo, we expanded the scope of our project, and with a color-coded spreadsheet tab or five, we formed a Resipiscence community of heartbeats deeply invested in an array of faith rooted social justice activism across the U.S.

Resipiscence is defined as a "change of mind or heart, reformation, a return to a sane, sound, or corrected view or position" (Merriam-Webster). The contributors within these pages are absolutely calling for a change of both mind and heart in the way we love or do not love our neighbor. In light of the national political tone, sanctioned state violence, a dehumanizing stance on immigration, and the prison industrial slave complex, a resolute call for a return to a corrected view of what and who made, makes, and will make this country great is our moral and theological responsibility.

In the 2018 edition, we reached out to those connected to us, and through invitation, curated a spiral bound Lenten Devotional that wrestled with the biblical texts from the perspective of a melanated Jesus that was murdered by the state and with how black and brown bodies were experiencing a perpetual Good Friday of state violence in America. Where was our resurrection Sunday? With the cover image of a black Jesus on the cross, a crown of thorns atop his locs and the symbolic use of red, green, and black, we centered directly impacted voices and expanded the faith narrative of Lent, or rather returned to an exploration of its infinite implicative possibilities.

What began as a small project turned into a resource used by several seminaries and conferences, many small groups, and hundreds of individuals to reflect on this sacred season in more depth, context, and breadth of narrative. We produced a weekly podcast that featured the contributors and connected their written expression to their lived experiences, faith narratives, and the local context for their liberative movement work.

With the cover image of Black power fists in a range of metallic colors, this year's edition is unapologetically much of the same. Told we met a need, we hope to continue creating a pathway that leads to personal, interpersonal, and systemic dismantling of white supremacy in our minds, hearts, bodies, families, faith, and faith communities. We sent out a national call for submissions and now have some contributors that Nichola and I have only met through their written theological explorations, calls to action, and laments. The podcast will be daily this time, offering greater depth of opportunity for daily devotion in the content and delving into the writer as well as their words. The *Resipiscence* contributors plan to meet together in the fall, connecting in person, gathering with other movement-oriented folks, broadening community and getting in these justice streets together.

These heartbeats are my tribe, and it is my hope that their expressions of lament, call to actively love ourselves and the least of these, challenge to consider an alternative perspective, wrestling with the text, and examination of privilege, proximity to power, and sacrifice, inspire you as they have inspired me: to move in my faith.

Vahisha Nabeehah Hasan
    ~meaning life, noble prophet, and to make things better in Arabic
    ~God's image
    ~Violet's only begotten daughter
    ~Nichola's Book-Baby-Mama

INTRODUCTION

Welcome to the 2019 edition of *Resipiscence: A Lenten Devotional for Dismantling White Supremacy*!

I am so excited that we releasing our second edition of this devotional. It touches a very deep longing in me.

For years, Lent has felt to me like a potentially revolutionary time that never lives up to its promise. I believe that all of us who take Lent seriously do so because we are longing for something—deeper connection, intimacy, wholeness, presence, love…and I am coming to understand that no number of years of giving up chocolate or television for 40 days is going to get us there. The change that we need is deeper and more relational than that. That means we can't get there on our own.

The holistic wellness that we long for comes from being in right relationship with each other, ourselves, and the created world, as well as with God. We long to be "right-sized" parts of a larger and very beautiful interdependent network of life. That is who we are created to be.

White supremacy is one of the most deeply entrenched obstacles to being in right relationship. We spend all of our days marinating in a stew of false ideas about who we are relative to other members of the human family and other parts of the created world, ideas that are reinforced by the systems and structures that govern our lives. Some of us are continually reminded that we are inferior; others of us are given the message that we are superior, and whether or not we are conscious of this training, it infects our relationships with one another and sabotages our attempts to work together for collective liberation.

The ways that these white supremacist messages are instilled are many; the distortions of our behavior are complex and nuanced; and the effects are deadly. White supremacy kills.

White supremacy is sinful. It disconnects us from God and from the interdependent human family and created world. It thwarts human thriving in ways that are often brutal and devastating.

This Lent, we have the opportunity to reflect deeply on the ways that this sin has infected our lives and our communities, and we have the opportunity to repent.

I know these words are loaded—*sin, repentance.* They have been used like weapons to shame people—often people who are already vulnerable systemically; in recent years, they have been employed especially to target LGBTQ people. But these words were meant to be engaged by *communities* to reflect on the ways that *they, collectively,* were missing the mark. Scripture is written not to individuals but to communities, and it emerges out of a culture that better understood our interdependence. The word *repentance* means "to turn and walk a different way," not on your own but as part of a community of similarly yearning souls.

So this Lent, we invite you to be part of the RESIPISCENCE community. We have gathered here a widely ranging collection of daily reflections from a very diverse group of contributors—diverse in identities, theologies, and experiences—and every one of them has something to say about how we dismantle white supremacy and all the institutions, laws, policies, habits, and ideologies that perpetuate it. The book is organized by week, and each section contains seven reflections on the scriptures for the following Sunday.

This book was created in 2019 and follows the Lenten lectionary for Year C. It is a collaborative project of Movement in Faith, Transform Network, Seminary of the Street, and Showing Up For Racial Justice (SURJ)—Faith.

More than anything, it emerges out of deep relationality. The people who contributed to this book are people Vahisha and I know, love, and labor alongside, as well as people who were recommended by our people. It has been a great joy to work with these writers, and especially with my co-editor, my book baby-mama, my sister from another mother, Vahisha Hasan, who is brilliant, funny, visionary, and extremely savvy with the Google spreadsheets!

May the labors represented by these pages and the communal reflections that emerge from them lead us toward the longed-for resurrection!

Nichola Torbett

First Sunday in Lent

LUKE 4:1-13

If You Worship Me: The Idol of White Supremacy and the Atrophy of the Soul

When Jesus asked his disciples, "What does it profit a man to gain the whole world and lose his soul?" he must've recalled the experience of being tempted by the devil. In the desert, Satan "led him up to a high place and showed him in an instant all the kingdoms of the world and said to him, 'I will give you all their authority and splendor … If you worship me, it will all be yours.'"

W.E.B. DuBois pondered this bargain in his essay, "The Souls of White Folk." Asking in a tone as if rhetorical, "But what on earth is whiteness that one should so desire it?" his answer is a retelling of this scripture for our time: "Whiteness is the ownership of the earth forever and ever, Amen!" What DuBois considered then is what we know now - that whiteness is but a social construct born from the bloody afterbirth of colonialism. It was created as a stronghold to keep and maintain the ill-gotten gains of European plunder all over the world.

It is not necessary to call white people "devils" to acknowledge the evil of white supremacy. Yet, to truly understand the evil of white supremacy requires one to confront the problem of white identity. Such confrontation is the realization that white identity is based in the perpetual violent subjugation of people of color.

That realization requires addressing what can only be understood as a spiritual schizophrenia that enables white people to experience privilege in a world social arrangement that is rooted in the pillage that DuBois identifies in his essay. This is a question that white Christians must confront for it lies at the very heart of understanding the corrosion of conscience that has crippled white people's collective capacity to "do unto others as you would have them do unto you." Whiteness has been made into an idol to be worshipped, raised up on a scaffold of lies and falsehoods told and retold to every generation.

Maintaining the arrangement of power and control invested in white identity requires all institutions in the society to uphold the fundamental lies that keep the identity in place. The role of the church in this process is crucial. Rather than call white people to confession, repentance and reparations, the church has worked as handmaiden to the system of white supremacy. This has been true since the day Columbus set sail with the blessing of the Church and a mandate from the Pope to conquer and take possession in the name of Jesus Christ. This has been true since the day the Church of England burned their name into the backsides of the Africans they bought and sold. It was the missionary, not the soldier, that paved the way for the conquistador and the colonizer. This historic truth has been crystallized in this oft-quoted African proverb, "When the white man came, he had the Bible and we had the land. He taught us to pray with our eyes closed. When we opened our eyes, we had the Bible and he had the land." As Jesus was tempted in the desert, the Christian church has bowed down to the spirit of white supremacy and gained the whole world. Consequently, the souls of white folk are in a constant state of atrophy.

For John the Baptist, repentance is an indictment on injustice and inequality. For the white church to be reconciled to the God it claims, it must first reconcile itself to its past and confess to the ways it has bowed down and worshipped white supremacy. It must then be involved in the restoration of the very communities it aided in oppressing. This is a work that goes beyond charity to structural change. In addition to confessing to the evils of its past, it must also confront and redress the evils of the present in which we witness a white church giving its blessing to soldiers at the border readying to make war on migrants; a white church providing sanctuary to cops who prey on people of color throughout this nation. Once it confesses the sins of the past and the present, then it will be on the path of redemption toward becoming a church of God, prepared to help white folk heal their crippled souls by renouncing an identity born in bloodshed for an identity reborn in right relationship with the rest of humanity and the One who created and loves us all.

Ewuare X. Osayande *is a social justice activist, poet and the author of several books including* Whose America?: New & Selected Poems *and* Commemorating King: Speeches Honoring the Civil Rights Movement. *With 25 years experience as an anti-oppression educator, he is the founder of Freedom Plow, an intersectional anti-racism workshop process for churches and non-profits. His forthcoming book is entitled* Blessed are Black Lives. *Learn more about him and his work at Osayande.org.*

DEUTERONOMY 26:1-11

Broken Liberators, Broken Liberation

It is truly a glorious moment when God tells the Israelites, after having witnessed their four centuries of brutal slavery ending in divine vengeance, that they will be given a new land "as an inheritance to possess" (26:1). And then to be with your people, everyone singing of how God "brought [you] into this place and gave [you] this land, a land flowing with milk and honey" (26:9). And as your bones mend, your muscles ease and heal, and with your newly returning strength, you then "celebrate the bounty that the LORD your God has given to you and to your house" (26:11) as this glorious new life begins.

But now imagine that you hear these celebrations, these shouts, not from your *own* kin, but from a foreign people coming over the hills, that local gossip says has just come from Egypt – and that the land that their foreign god promised them – possession of which they are already *singing* about – is *your* land.

This is the terrifying point made by Osage scholar and University of Kansas professor Robert Allen Warrior in his brief but devastating article "Canaanites, Cowboys, and Indians: Deliverance, Conquest, and Liberation Theology Today." Penned nearly 30 years ago, Warrior hones in on the oft-ignored 'dark side' of the Exodus of the Israelites from Egypt – the massacre and displacement of the indigenous Canaanites. Warrior begins that since "[a] delivered people is not a free people, nor is it a nation," of necessity then they need a 'new' land before they can claim to be either. In order to make this 'promised land' possible, then, "Yahweh the deliverer [becomes] Yahweh the conqueror," and "the same power used against the enslaving Egyptians" is then redirected "to defeat the indigenous inhabitants of Canaan." So the god of the Israelites denounces the Canaanites as "wicked," with "[a] religion... to be avoided at all costs" and warns that they "are not [even] to be trusted, nor are they to be allowed to enter into social relationships with the people of Israel" (Exodus 12:31b-33). Then as with any *Endlösung*, any final solution, God condemns countless generations of Canaanites to dispossession and death, commanding the Israelites to "utterly destroy them;... [to] make no covenant with them, and [to] show no mercy to them" (Deuteronomy 7:2).

For Warrior, as a Native American and scholar, any study of Exodus that avoids "those parts of the story that describe Yahweh's command to mercilessly annihilate the indigenous population [of Canaan]" is deliberately misleading. And though this reminder truly ravages the most inspiring liberation story of all time, by so tearing into our glorious, activist narratives he leaves us with precious wisdom: every would-be liberator is a would-be colonizer, *especially if we are willfully ignorant of history's reminders of a liberated people's own capacity for domination.*

It makes sense, too.

Like the traumatized Israelites who suffered under 400 years of slavery, we who fight and have been victimized by white supremacy and its spawn can never completely free ourselves from its ability to infect our vision and deeds. So be it through community, therapy or prayer, Christian activists must be ever vigilant lest trauma from white supremacy possess us anew, transforming us into our former oppressors–in ways great and small–making us more hungry for dominance than freedom, prioritizing raw power over healing.

Because woe be upon us if we, like the newly-liberated Israelites, ever reap harvests on stolen land, fattening ourselves on foundation money while lording it over those we are supposed to serve. Woe be to our labors if we ignore the voices of the elders and children who God has charged with guiding us. And heaven help us if we set ourselves up as priests of the Holy One–impressing the public with our flowing robes– while we simultaneously make neighborhood children "pass through the fire" (2 Kings 21:6) and so slake our own ambition and greed with the blood of their futures.

So keep awake, friends (Mark 13:37) lest we inspire others to pray for liberation from us as we once prayed for liberation from others. Honor our calling and our dead by saving others from the fate we endured, not by inflicting it upon those whom we love and lead.

Francisco Herrera studied viola and orchestra conducting in Kansas City, Missouri and Geneva, Switzerland before entering seminary in 2006. He received his M.Div. from Chicago Theological Seminary in 2012 and is now a PhD student at the Lutheran School of Theology at Chicago. Francisco also works as a seminary instructor in theology and Spanish, composes worship and devotional music, blogs at www.loveasrevolution.blogspot.com, tweets at @PolyglotEvangel, and relishes his duties as the Convener of #decolonizeLutheranism.

LUKE 4:1-13

The gospel according to white folks

The thing about white folks and the Bible
is that we always put ourselves
in the role of Jesus
(or Good Samaritan, Prodigal Parent,
soil with the most manure)

so when the Temptation roles around
we see the devil face to face
and it doesn't appear to be a mirror.

To the stone-into-bread pitch
we answer affirmative,
not because we are often hungry,
but because we want the naming rights
... even to giving.

We could feed the hungry world,
and be recognized as so caring
without ever getting up to our elbows
in our own flour and yeast,
after all, stone dust
is the original genetically modified.

All the authority? Seriously?
Of course it's a "yes."
We can fake the devil-worship --
power is always worth it
and we can fix the means later
on somebody else's bent-over beat end.

The dopamine rush is being in charge
of course, only for good,
and we are the most qualified
to see the overview

though soon we will delegate
some tasks to others
and acknowledge them publicly.

Third is a little jumpstart to safety,
and we are owed —
children free of cancer,
and parents free of dementia,
homes safe from wildfire and hurricane,
and no pain, never any pain.

Now all we have to do
is find a vein
and if our needle plunge from a pinnacle
gets too deadly we can rename it
from "war" to "epidemic"
and talk healing, not incarceration.

The thing about white folks and the Bible
is that we love the wilderness.

It is not so much a retreat,
as a platform for coalition with the Tempter.

Maren C. Tirabassi *is white. Her most recent book is* A Child Laughs – Prayers for Justice and Hope, *an anthology with seventy-seven writers from eleven countries. She is a guest preacher, new author mentor, and workshop facilitator with prison inmates, new English speakers, and cancer and dementia patients.*

blog: giftsinopenhands@wordpress.com
Facebook, Casa: An Experiment in Doing Church Online, RevGalsBlogPals

ISAIAH 58

A Call to Mend: Fasting for Justice

This has been a year of disbelief and growing despondency for many in the United States.

As a clinical social worker who has made it her life's work to look at humanity through the lenses of emotional wellness and our connection to spirit, I find it hard to accept that this is how life should be now and for generations to come. Within us is a pulse, a heartbeat for the collective. We have the capacity to be part of God's mending. This is the call I find in Isaiah 58, which is written to people returning from exile and eager for God to vanquish their enemies. And they are wondering why it's not happening.

Like any good professor, if everyone fails a test, God reteaches, rehashes and gives examples of the materials needed in order to produce the results desired. Basically, God gave the people the answers to the test in this passage. The issue presented in the text appears to be that the people were unaware of the level of authenticity, vulnerability and acquisition of "resurrectional" qualities and tools required.

There are places that encourage this authenticity, vulnerability, and resurrection, even if they are not in our traditional church settings, i.e. anonymous meetings, protests, board meetings, classrooms, hallways students who are tired of hurting, and living rooms full of souls gathered for the purpose of healing the community.

I am the leader of Mending Life Concepts Empowerment Group, a nonprofit meeting people at the intersection of spirituality and emotional wellness. We want to help people mend! This concept of mending, for me, was best understood while I worked in the area of forensic social work and substance abuse recovery.

In that work, I learned that God provides covering for those who push back from the instant gratification and numbing of addiction, those who are willing to feel the pain, walk through it, and emerge with wisdom for those who will come after them. In 2018 we would say "God's got your back" as you seek to heal. When people cry out honestly, God hears and and is moved. The crying out requires work--introspective work, emotional regulation, ability to tolerate distress, and mindfulness of who you are and your own significance on the earth.

There is a process within the 12 steps that requires an individual to "make amends," finding the places in their lives that can be repaired and also locating the areas that need to be accepted as unbendable and that will only shift if it is God's will and God's doing: "God grant me the serenity to accept the things I cannot change; courage to change the things I can; and wisdom to know the difference."

So why are we called to mend? Isn't it God's job to heal? Won't Jesus fix it? That is what the song writer said…right? I have searched the text and even bargained with spirit to "fix it" for me in times past. I have yet to find in the text where it tells me that God will fix all of my problems, flying in on a chariot with magical unicorns sprinkling glittering healing dust across the land because I asked God to do so. Nope, none of this can I find, and per Isaiah 58, the work of the mender belongs to those who seek justice in their fast.

This is a kind of fasting that requires a death—death to the old ways and embrace of the new. We release ourselves from the lies of perfection into spaces of seeing hurt as part of the human experience. A part that allows us to remain connected and gives us power to lift one another up and help each other carry our crosses.

Fasting for justice and causing the universe to bend in its direction requires the work of humanity and communal righteousness. We must push past the acquired traditions that have now become everyday practice. In our numbness, we have lost the ear of God in walking in ways that do not belong to us and refusing to look inward prior to calling out. This text reminds us that we have power as we are made in the image of Elohim. We must seek ways to create justice with the backing of God. A call to mend requires work, not just begging for magical hyper-spiritual moments that often lead to destruction. These moments include regaining access to the bond of humanity and remembering that we are all connected by spirit. What better season than this, when we acknowledge the weight of the cross and the joy of watching God join us in our righteous mending!

Margaret Conley *is the owner of MLC Consulting, LLC and the President of Mending Life Concepts Empowerment Group, Inc., where the focus of care is directed toward serving underprivileged populations at the intersection of spirituality and emotional wellness. Margaret has produced an evidence-based, clinically aligned, theological model designed for use by clergy, academics and clinicians to help lead the conversation around faith-based trauma in individual and community settings.*

MATTHEW 6:1-6, 16-24

Looking for Treasure

I am looking for treasure. What is my treasure? I am looking for life abundant. What does abundant life look like in a world where so many lives are being destroyed?

I am tired. At 25, I know that I am very young, but I am still tired. I am an activist; I am a writer. I've been involved in "movement work" for a very short time, but I am still tired.

I desire abundant life because I am tired of how the current world interacts with me. For many of us, working towards a new world means sacrifice of our time, our energy. It can mean extending ourselves so that our emotional, mental, physical and spiritual health is at risk. Sacrifices are made, but I want to make sure that I am making the right sacrifices. I don't want to sacrifice joy. If I do, why am I doing this work? For me, joy is one of my treasures. And joy is part of abundant life for me.

What are the things that give me joy? When I am able to connect with others over food and drink, when I am able to laugh and have fun with others during this fight for our lives. For me, joy is play and delight in other people. Joy is just relationships. For me, the presence of justice in my relationships is how I know that I am being loved well.

The love of Jesus becomes so deeply abstracted in many Christian circles. That is why so many of us involve ourselves in racial justice--as one means to love people of color. So many of us strive to pursue justice. But sometimes we forget why we do justice work to begin with.

Since I do racial justice work, I meet a lot of white folks who are well versed in how social justice is part of Jesus' ministry. I mentioned that doing this work has made me tired. One of the reasons why I feel tired is because I often see white folks perform anti-racism work as if they are investing in their own social reputation or image. They seem to put their energy into appearing "good" rather than dismantling white supremacy and encouraging healing. They want someone to notice their good deeds. But, do they really desire justice and healing? It makes me wonder where their heart and treasure truly lie.

Even as a Black woman among fellow change-makers of color, there can be a temptation to do things for celebrity, for reputation, to become revered for what we do. Being so concerned with how I appeared to others, I've had moments when I have lost sight of what I really wanted in this life: to flourish and be part of a beloved community. This is why I do social justice, because I want these things, and I recognize that others want to flourish, too. I am fighting for our chance at abundant life.

That we might concern ourselves with social status and celebrity in the midst of a world dying to flourish shows me how much we have been trained by the world to desire those things which we don't need. We are told by our culture that what matters most is that we are more important than someone else--and that if we are not, we must seek to be.

I myself have felt so much pressure to have to offer credentials to be perceived as valuable. Often, white folks and men won't begin to even acknowledge my efforts or existence unless I drop familiar names, conferences, cohorts, seminaries. Unless I show them what programs and speaking engagements I have involved myself in, there may be no incentive for them to get to know me as a person. I might get reduced to how much of a "resource" I am, whether I can be used as social capital. Some circles can become all about capital.

And when it becomes about capital, my everyday attempts to bring flourishing and healing don't matter. My commitment to integrity in all things doesn't matter. The words of courage and solidarity whispered to loved ones in moments of crisis, they do not matter. None of it matters, for it is not the treasure a capitalist, white supremacist culture looks for.

For Lent, I want us to consider: when we do work, what are we investing in? What do we call "treasure" with our lives?

Rachel Virginia Hester *is a queer, Afro-Latina photographer, writer and Christian activist living in the southern United States. Rachel has been a part of leadership cohorts such as Soulforce's South East House Fellowship and Union Theological Seminary's Millennial Leadership Project. She is passionate about woman of color feminist literature, nature and friendship. When Rachel isn't taking photographs, she can be found practicing instruments or munching on oatmeal cookies.*

Website: thegenerouspine.com
Facebook: @rachelpinephotography
Instagram: @rae_virginia
Twitter: @rachelvirginiah

DEUTERONOMY 26:1-11

No Monkeys Allowed

"Grampa," sobbed the little one, "Why don't they want me to be at their party?"

"Lisa, sometimes people just say mean things. I'm sure it wasn't somthin' you did."

"No, that's not it. I thought Monica was my friend!" yelled Lisa, "She said 'Sorry Lisa, no monkeys allowed,' and then her and the other girls started laughing."

Taken aback, Stuart said "Don't you worry; I'll get to the bottom of this. I'll be back in a little while."

Stuart grabbed his keys to drive over talk to Monica's father, Nate; he wondered how and why Monica would treat Lisa that way when they have always enjoyed spending time together--swimming at the lake, going to barbeques, singing to Justin Bieber, and watching late night movies. It had been a while since Stuart had seen Nate, but he sees Nate's father almost every Sunday at church. And they often reflect after service on the time they spent in the foxholes in Korea.

As Stuart pulls up to Nate's house, he sees him piddling around in the flat-bed of his 4x4.

"Nate! What you up to?" Stuart said.

"Ah, nothing much just taking a look at this ridin'mower… looking for my wrench."

"I wanted to talk with you about this party for Monica…Lisa said she couldn't come."

Nate stopped searching for his tools and looks up at Stuart, "You know, to be honest, I'm surprised that's the reason you showed up. My daddy told me that your daughter April and some coon from up north had Lisa. Why you let your daughter marry some Black man is beyond me, but if you think I'm going to let her be around my daughter and influence her with that liberal garbage, yer' crazy."

"Lisa is a good girl! I know your daddy didn't raise you like this! Yo' daddy and I served with Blacks and whites together!" pleaded Stuart. "What you are doing…"

Nate interrupted, "You tryin' to preach to me? I heard you and Daddy growing up saying 'Blacks better be careful', and 'they should know their place.' Now since we know your daughter is married to one, you think your granddaughter ain't one of them? Naw, she's still Black even if she don't look it!"

Stuart had never seen this disdain in Nate's eyes before. As Stuart drove away disillusioned, he thought of what he previously thought was Fake News, a media concoction; the concept of white privilege. He wondered if it was true then, how much it determined how he was viewed; was he really deserving of all the military decorations he received, the corporate promotions? Why weren't other ethnic groups considered as frequently? Nate's bigotry made Stuart reconsider if he even viewed his granddaughter as white.

As Stuart drove, he decided to stop by a church that he had never attended before--the African Methodist Episcopal Zion Church in Durham. As he walked into the church, he saw a man who was cleaning the pulpit. "Excuse me, could you direct me to the pastor?" asked Stuart. "Sure," replied the man as he put down the broom and approached, "That's me. What can I do for you?"

As Stuart explained the situation, the pastor's face became serious. "Let's have a seat," offered the pastor. Stuart retold his granddaughter's horrors and his own complicity with racism. The Black pastor looked up and said, "I know that you want to make it easier for your granddaughter. What you can do is celebrate her uniqueness. Let me tell you a story. Deuteronomy 26:1-11 instructs the Children of Israel when they enter the Promised Land, to give an offering of the first fruits of their new land. They rejoiced in the Lord and with the Levite priests and with the foreigners accompanying them. Giving first fruits ensured that all of God's children benefited from the blessing of the land, even those who didn't look like them, because they remembered that at one time they were oppressed by the Egyptians. Stuart, as you give up white privilege, and celebrate your granddaughter's multiethnic heritage, you will empower her, and you will be free in the Lord to worship God in truth."

"Can we pray for that?" asked Stuart.

———○————————————————————————————————○———

Taiwo Stevenson *is a man with integrity, wisdom, and a desire to see God's kingdom advanced in the lives of all people. He began a campus ministry called Kingdom U at Virginia State University in 2010 and has written a book called* Kingdom Dynamics: A Practical Guide to Discipleship *in 2013. He is a recent graduate of the Samuel DeWitt Proctor School of Theology at Virginia Union University and a 2018 contributor to RESIPISCENCE.*

Twitter: @DaRealWoo
Instagram: @woodaddy3

PSALM 91:1-2, 9-16

Hush Arbor Day

In her book, Joy Unspeakable: contemplative practices of the Black church, *scholar Barbara Holmes mentions hush arbors—"slave-initiated places of refuge and communal worship."*

Can you see them?

Sweat drips down his forehead and stings his eyes as he labors in the fields. But he dares not pause, despite the aching curl of his back. There's too much at stake, no reason to catch the whip today.

Another, her skin tawny, creamier even than Georgia red clay, finds her fingers raw from the picking. The master had not even bothered to force her into the house, a grace like the scent of magnolia's blooms.

The plantation was not large enough to warrant many slaves, and they are only a few more in number, their overseer, lackluster, and stupid to boot.

He dozes in the red maple's shade, legs crossed in front of his potato-shaped body, the bill of a brown leather hat pulled over his eyes. Their silence, a signal, was good fodder For his dreams of being at home with his own family, his wife's corn fritters and the chance to catch a few fish to fry—all he really hopes for.

Can you hear them?

Their feet know how to skim the ground, barely
making a sound above the northern mockingbird, calling its mate.
They make their way to the edge of the field and into the vines,
holy ground.

Their hopes are greater, the taste of freedom all over God's
breath that blew through the brush. The hush arbor in the muscadine
vines, the place to gather and whisper of joys unspeakable, of
God's visioned promised land, maybe up North or out West.
This day their silence
A signal to meet in that secret place,
the shelter, where the ground held space for bent knees,
a sweeter communion because this was a choice no white could sour,
no thing
could break their trust that God would meet them there.

And God did. They caught glimpses of their own migration,
Their children's children sprouting in the fertile ground of Harlem,
a fresh
Renaissance, a community in love with its beauty and flourishing.
When happiness bubbled up from their gut, they could not help but
share it with shout.

The hush arbors, a sanctuary, held space for it all, holding us even now
without a shadow of a doubt. What will God show us next? Perhaps a
salvation beyond our
reckoning, perhaps a power greater than our wildest dreams.
Even God's shadow falling through light in the vines can do that.

Jasmin Morrell *is a writer for* The Porch Magazine *and an MFA student in the Grady School of Journalism at the University of Georgia. She's festival producer for the Movies and Meaning Festival, and she's served as Communications Director for the Wild Goose Festival, as well as a day shelter for people experiencing homelessness. Jasmin is passionate about the power of story and imagination to foster collective and individual healing and currently calls Asheville, North Carolina home.*

Second Sunday
in Lent

LUKE 9:28-30

The Prophetic Possibilities of Prayer

"...**Jesus took with him Peter and John and James**, and went up on the mountain to pray. **And while** *he* **was praying**...Suddenly they saw two men, **Moses and Elijah, talking to him**." (Luke 9: 28-30, emphasis mine)

White-supremacist-capitalist-patriarchy commodifies and privatizes everything. Our religious sentiment bears this imprint. As such, we've reconstructed a loving and liberating God as a genie that appears when we rub a "prayer lamp." This white supremacist (grand) wizard emerges to grant our three wishes of prosperity, power, and public notoriety.

To the contrary, reclaiming an afro-centric, Black, revolutionary and liberating Jesus offers a much better platform of engagement with prayer.

Jesus and his homies head to Mountaintop Missionary Baptist Church and a prayer service kicks off. According to Mark, service got so good Peter didn't want to leave. But the purpose of the prayer service was not to name and claim a blessing or breakthrough via radical individualism. Jesus was mindful to take some people to worship with him. The revolutionary Jesus sees worship as a communal venture that is best experienced with others who are committed to a common cause of collective freedom.

Jesus, Peter, James and John host a prayer service. In this vein, prayer serves as a foundational platform of inspiration and instruction that undergirds us for impending conflicts that lie in wait at the foot of the mountains of our lives. In other words, we pray as part of preparing for battle. That's why Jesus should've taken some Black women with him. Black women know how to get a prayer through. Sistaz know how to prepare for battle.

But, according to Luke, Jesus took three brothers and (as good as Peter said service was) we can't even verify that anyone other than Jesus offered up a prayer.

Luke says, "And while *he* was praying" not "while *they* were praying." This implies, although they went up there with Jesus, even his closest disciples can be so contaminated by oppressive ideologies that we sit back and watch Jesus perform instead of participating in the work with him.

Nevertheless, Jesus prayed. And while *he* was praying, the prayer changed him.

When we center a more communal approach to prayer it changes us.

But, it also invites us into a more intimate relationship with our ancestors. While Jesus was praying, suddenly everybody saw two men, Moses and Elijah. The ancestors showed up. People who had been engulfed in the same struggle, who shared a similar heritage and lineage, arrive at the place where somebody was praying.

White supremacist theology demands we denounce ancestral worship as demonic. Yet, this text unapologetically connects Jesus with forerunners in the faith; prophetic predecessors upon whose symbolic shoulders he now stands. And, luckily, because Jesus was community-minded, even the prayer-less disciples got to experience this affirming encounter.

It means something significant for us to be able to draw from and summon the power of our predecessors. That's a function of prayer. It is much more than simply evoking the presence of God and asking for favor(s). Prayer ought to move us from a me-centered cosmology to a we-centered theology.

Moses and Elijah show up and talk to Jesus. It doesn't get much Blacker than that.

Some scholars suggest that Moses represents the Law and Elijah represents the prophets. Those interpretations are plausible but not persuasive. What I believe they represent are notable figures in the great cloud of witnesses. I also believe they weren't the only ancestors who showed up. Redactors and editors have likely written women out of this ancestral encounter, much like we've done with Black women's contributions to more contemporary iterations of the freedom movement. But I'm sure they were there. I bet Hagar, Deborah, Rahab and Ruth were on that mountain. And I'm sure Jesus talked to them and they talked to him.

These prayerful, mountaintop moments are what fuel our fire for freedom fighting. And we must always call upon and acknowledge the presence, power, and peace offered from our prophetic predecessors. And let us call ALL of them in prayer. Let's call Frederick Douglas AND Henry Highland Garnet; David Walker AND Nat Turner; Harriet Tubman

AND Sojourner Truth; Pauli Murray AND Jarena Lee; James Cone AND Albert Cleage; our forefathers AND our foremothers; Northeast Africa AND West and South Africa.

These are the types of prayers I long for. These are the prayers that motivate us on the mountaintop and lead us into victory in the valley.

*Sought after for his perspectives on spirituality, social justice, and contemporary culture, **Earle J. Fisher** earned a Bachelor of Science Degree in Computer Science from LeMoyne-Owen College and a Master of Divinity Degree from Memphis Theological Seminary. He served on the Pastoral staff at the Miss. Blvd Christian Church as an Associate Minister for two years where he earned the title "Pastor Cool." In 2018 Pastor Earle earned a Doctor of Philosophy in Communication from the University of Memphis and currently serves as Senior Pastor of Abyssinian Baptist Church in Memphis, Tennessee.*

Dr. Fisher is an Adjunct Instructor of Religion and Humanities professor at several local colleges in Memphis. He was selected as an outstanding UNCF Historically Black College and University (HBCU) alumnus and inducted in the 2012 Hall of Honors class. He is a proud member of Alpha Phi Alpha, husband of one wife, Denise, father of one son, Jalen, believer in one God, and friend and mentor to many.

PSALM 27

Light My Way

The Lord is my light,
The light that brightens the path.
Traveling by caravan
Traveling with small children
Traveling alone with thoughts in our hearts of those left behind
Traveling in the cold dark night
Fear for safety, hungry and afraid
Yet we press on in search of freedom and safety.

The Lord is my light
And my salvation
Salvation from persecution
Salvation from poverty
Salvation from violence in my home country

The Lord is my light and my salvation
Whom shall I fear?
Fear the military police at the border?
Being stopped?
Being detained?
Sheltered in camps?
Separation from children?
Silver foiled blankets?
Cages?
To be treated like criminals?
Whom shall I fear?

When those of evil intent seek to assault and to tear me apart,
Rip my children from my arms
—Even my adversaries and opposers will stumble and fall
No matter the army which stands at the border to block my path
My heart beating deep within my flesh
Each pulse quickening with each forward step
Though patrols will increase and threats of deportation

My heart won't fear.
I will be confident.

There's only one thing I've asked the Lord
The one thing I've searched for
To find sanctuary in the house of the Lord for the remainder of my life
To look upon his beauty and to inquire in his temple
For the Lord will hide me
He will give me asylum in the day of trouble
I will offer in his tent sacrifices with praise
I will sing and make melody to the Lord

So Lord when we cry to you
Weary from our walking
Tired, hungry, thirsty
Lord be gracious and answer me!
Answer my cries!
For my heart says Come seek his face
Lord, it's your face I seek

Lord, I plead my case for asylum
Lord hear my cause for my cause is just
Don't hide your face from looking at me
Don't turn your servants away in anger
Lord, you have been my help.
Don't leave me.
Don't forsake me, God, my salvation
Even if my father and mother leave me
Lord you will take me up

We have traveled far
Stony roads
Threat of thieves
Attacks in the night
No protection
No shelter from the storm
Lord teach me your way
Lead me on a level path
Because of my enemies
Because of my foes
Because of my adversaries
Don't give me up
For false accusers rise to call me a rapist

They rise to call me a drug dealer
They rise to call me criminal
They rise to call me a gangsta
They breathe out violence

I believe
Still, believe
Yet to believe
Hope and believe
I will see the goodness of the Lord;
In this land of promise,
In this land of the free,
In this home of the brave.
I will see the goodness of the Lord in the land of the living.

Families will wait.
Neighbors will wait.
Fathers and mothers will wait.
Children will wait.
We will wait for the Lord.
Our hearts will be strong.
We will take courage.
We will wait on the Lord.

Monica Leak is the editor and a contributing writer of Faith of our Founders 100 Daily Devotionals to Inspire, Encourage and Propel the Finer Woman. She contributed writings for The Road to Calvary Surviving a Season of Suffering, a Lenten devotional and to Resipiscence: A Lenten Devotional for Dismantling White Supremacy. She is a school based speech-language pathologist in Maryland, a librarian for the John Leland Center for Theological Studies where she is also a student and an associate minister at First Baptist Church Vienna.

Monica Leak on Instagram and Facebook
MoPrayer on Twitter

PSALM 27

"Speak!"

Mass incarceration, racism, police brutality, shrinking middle class, voter intimidation, immigration abuse, war on the poor--the list can go on, naming things that make this world feel dark and unwelcoming. This is especially true for people of color. Much of our history is cloaked in the darkness of racism and abuse, yet as Christians we are called to be a light in this world. The season of Lent serves as a time of reflection on our relationship with God as we prepare for Easter. But, how do we reflect light in a time that seems filled with darkness?

"The Lord is my light and my salvation; whom shall I fear? The Lord is the refuge of my life of whom shall I be afraid?" These strong words open Psalm 27, a song attributed to King David. This psalm is meant to instill confidence and hope in God as we face dire situations in life. The words of light, salvation, and strength are supposed to give us the confidence to keep going in the face of injustices that we see and feel every day. The question is, can these words written thousands of years ago really help us to face our problems today? Or are they just words we read at certain times of the year and then continue to live in fear of what we see? I am reminded of the kids' game where they say "Sticks and stones may break my bones, but words will never hurt me." If this is true, then it could also mean that words will never help us either.

That jeer is not true, however. Words can indeed hurt, and so that means they can also help. The right word can encourage us to keep going just as the wrong word can make us stop dead in our tracks. We are living in a time where the power of words is so strong that those in charge are trying to silence and censor. It is no coincidence that the leaders of this country, conspiring with monied interests, are trying to silence the free press. This is the same tactic used over and over by empires attempting to control the masses through words.

It is up to us to keep using our words, the right words to instill hope and action in our people. Throughout history, from the prophetic words of Amos to the freedom songs of today, words, whether spoken or sung, have the power to encourage and uplift a people to risk themselves for their community.

In this psalm, we are taken through the things that can come against us, but each time we are reminded to be confident that God will deliver. When they change the voter district to weaken the minority vote, speak words of confidence and keep fighting. When they criminalize drug addiction for some but not others, speak words of confidence and keep fighting. When we watch them plan and plot our demise using the court system, speak words of confidence and keep fighting.

This Lenten season the world may feel like it is hopelessly dark, but we must speak with confidence in the power of the light of God and the personhood of Jesus in our lives. The psalm concludes in verse 14 by reminding us to be strong, let our hearts take courage, and wait on the Lord. We must use our words of assurance, hope and confidence in God and ourselves to keep fighting for and with those whose words are not heard or valued. What are your words of confidence? And how will you use them to further freedom of others this season?

Rev. **Rochelle S. Andrews** is the CEO/President of The Vizion Group, which works with businesses, churches and nonprofits helping them to fulfill their mission. Rochelle is an ordained deacon in the African Methodist Episcopal Church. She spends much of her time working on policy, advocacy, and social justice to create educational and economic opportunities for underserved communities. She's also a foodie and a gadget geek.

Twitter - @chellecanhelp
Facebook - @theviziongroupllc
Instagram - @chellero94

PSALMS 27; LUKE 13:31-35

Rebuking Fear and Foxes

In the Lenten season, we are reminded that we are called to do ministry. We are called to a renewed focus of denying ourselves and to see what we can do for others. In short, we are called to do the work of the Lord. We are called to respond to that burning desire that we have inside of us to do what God has called us to do. It's during the Lenten season, that we take some time out and reflect on why we are here and what God would have us do.

I think about this a lot because I believe that I am not only called to pastor and to serve as a professor, but I am also called to do ministry in the streets. As a scholar/activist, this means that I find myself protesting and bearing witness to injustices happening in our community. Grounded in my theological beliefs, I also truly feel called to do this work. I tell others that I am standing with those who find themselves persecuted and on the margins because my faith teaches me to do so.

However, I have found that standing against the status quo and standing with those who have suffered at the hands of injustice is not as glamorous as some may think. The truth is that any time you take to the streets to protest and bear witness, there is a chance that you will lose friends and make enemies. You also can be arrested, beaten, tear gassed, or even worse—killed. Truthfully, many times, it's a scary proposition to stand knowing that law enforcement will meet you with tactical gear and military-styled weapons. It is this reality, grounded in our fear, that probably keeps many from joining in embodied solidarity with our neighbors who are suffering injustices.

The Psalmist wrote, "The Lord is my light and my salvation; whom shall I fear? The Lord is the stronghold of my life; of whom shall I be afraid?" Maybe this was the Psalm Jesus had in mind when he was on his way to Jerusalem. He knew what was waiting for him there, but still he went to confront the center of religious and political power. The word says that "at that same time some Pharisees came to Jesus and said, 'Leave this place and go somewhere else. Herod wants to kill you.' Instead of becoming fearful and taking the warning from the Pharisees and turning around, Jesus told them "'Go tell that fox, I will drive out demons and heal people today and tomorrow and on the third day I will reach my goal.'" In short, Jesus reminded them that he still had work to do.

Many people ask me why I do what I do. As I mentioned earlier, I feel called to this work. Whether some question my role or my motives, the reasons why I do what I do, to those who genuinely are concerned about my safety, I try to respond to my call. I still have work to do and while I understand fear to be a part of my call, I pray that it does not stop me from doing what God expects from me.

Rev. **Dr. Andre E. Johnson** is Senior Pastor of Gifts of Life Ministries in Memphis, Tennessee. He is also an Assistant Professor of Communication and Rhetoric, Race, Religion, and Media Studies at the University of Memphis. He serves as the Dr. Henry Logan Starks Fellow at Memphis Theological Seminary and Adjunct Faculty member of Homiletics, Black Preaching and Sacred Rhetoric at Christian Theological Seminary in Indianapolis, Indiana.

Facebook @AndreJohnson
Twitter and Instagram @aejohnsonphd
Website: http://www.aejohnsonphd.com/

GENESIS 15:1-6

The Ripples of Hope

I often wonder if any of the work that I do will have a result, if this work of protest will come to fruition and reflect the lines of the Lord's Prayer boldly proclaiming, "Thy kingdom come, thy will be done, on earth as it is in heaven." Instead, I often get discouraged, feel alienated, and find myself continuing to shout out in desperation from the margins.

It's not hard to feel discouraged. There are days when I wonder, "Is there any worth in my efforts? Or is trying to bring about a world of justice and equity as embodied in the flesh and blood of Christ some fleeting fantasy?" Because in these days, it feels like no matter how hard I try, I continue to bleed out from the micro and macro aggressions doled out by the powers and principalities of this world. In trying to live out the words of the Lord's Prayer, I feel some days that I would rather just stop, curl up, and let it all end. Sure, this sounds dramatic, but living as a person of color in a system that doesn't desire my existence or who God created me to be is tantamount to dying repeatedly.

Sometimes the powers and principalities of this world seem so big. Sometimes I feel like the demon of white supremacy is such an intoxicating drug that everyone under its influence would rather live a destructive and fragmented existence rather than have the opportunity to live life abundantly in community. Sometimes I just want to give into the effects of the drug, give into the systems of antiblackness, be regarded as "the model minority," a favored tool of the demon of white supremacy to drive a poisonous wedge of separation between communities of color, to further ensure the power of whiteness. To be seduced by the power of whiteness, to have the temptation dangled before me, to be drugged enough to forget that proximity to the power of whiteness does not equate to power itself.

But that's not the world that God created, and it is not the world that God intended for us.

I am thankful that if Abram had doubts about the word of the Lord, he didn't give into them. Even if Abram's descendants would number as much as the stars in the sky, Abram would not live to see them, and yet he acted on faith. This one conversation, this one promise, ripples throughout the course of history, impacting lives across time and generations. This promise, while it is given to an individual, is a promise of community. It is a promise of family. Even in the most troubling of times, it is a promise of hope.

The work that I do to fight against the oppressive powers of white supremacy and antiblackness is exhausting. This work may even take my life from me. And I know that I will not live to see the results of my labors. Then I remember Abram, and how the promise contained in the word of the Lord has rippled throughout human history. That bringing life to words is not restricted to a single moment or event in time, but expands far beyond what we can ever imagine. Even in the midst of my frustration and distress, I continue to hope. Hope can be risky and dangerous; the demons of this world want to wrest hope from our grasp. As a people of faith, we carry hope in our bones. The demons of this world are willing to shatter those bones and empty out the marrow. Yet I continue to hope, because hope is carried across time and generations.

I believe in an embodied hope that defies time and space. I believe in hope in the peculiar person of Christ. I remember hope in my baptism and the Eucharist. Baptism isn't about the individual, but it is about an individual being enfolded into the body of Christ. The Eucharist is being re-enfolded, time and time again, into that body.

Even when my hope wanes, I try to summon the energy to recall those who have trodden the path before us. They created a way so we can continue their holy work this day. May we continue to pray, and especially remember to hope, that our efforts are not in vain, but bring a continued path for those still to come. That they might live out the words, "Thy kingdom come, thy will be done on earth as it is in heaven" until they become a reality. May we always remember that we number the stars in the sky, and that God's work through our hands is never in vain.

*Rev. **Tuhina Verma Rasche** is an ordained pastor in the Evangelical Lutheran Church in America (ELCA) and is a frequent writer and speaker on the inter-sections of faith and race. She also has articles featured in* Inheritance Mag-azine, Bearings Magazine, *and a number of publications within the ELCA on preaching, spirituality, and identity.*

Twitter, Instagram, Facebook: @tvrasche
Medium: https://medium.com/@tvrasche
Blog: https://thislutheranlife.blogspot.com

LUKE 13:31-35

For Those Who Seek Freedom

These are the days that separate the courageous from the apathetic.
These are the days that separate the purposeful from the foolish.
These are the days that separate the loving from the fearful.
How will you spend your days?

For those who seek the freedom of all people, our daily work must be about healing and deliverance. Even with all that is required, day in and day out, in communities, churches, organizations and state houses, the repairing of humanity is ultimately spiritual work that must be attended to as rigorously as the more practical tactics and strategies that we employ.

God is calling us into greater alignment with God's will, calling us to go out and be the love that God has for each one of us. But remember that God's love is not always easy. God's love is there to both call us into the truth of who we are, and to soothe us when those truths are hard to face and harder to transform.

Notice that I did not say God's love is here to call us into the truth of who others are. God's grace asks us to look at ourselves, heal ourselves, grow ourselves, save ourselves and in our wholeness, call others into theirs. Are you willing to do the daily work of looking in the mirror? Are you willing to sit in a circle and face the truth of your own privilege while you invite others to do the same? Are you strong enough to see where you are in the way of the freedom you seek?

Jesus knew his work deeply and was so committed to it that no threat, no fate, no ridicule could deter him. As we fiercely ask others to embody the love of God, humility is our greatest ally. Our work for liberation is beautiful and daunting. You too will be challenged, threatened, questioned and denied, but for us, there is no greater obstacle to our divine path than ourselves. When uncertainty comes and courage is required, we must summon the courage that opens the heart, not the courage that emboldens the ego.

Our power to transform our communities lies in our power to transform ourselves. Be powerful enough to love yourself. Be powerful enough to be tender with yourself. Find the souls around you that see you clearly and accept your light and your shadows. Let them see the truth of who you are and invite them in to witness your wholeness. Care for each other, nurture each other, hold each other accountable, and together, go into battle for the things you know are worth fighting for.

*A cultural strategist, writer, and producer, **Anasa Troutman** has dedicated her work to the importance of culture and the power of love. As founder and CEO of her company, Culture Shift Creative, and the Executive Director of Historic Clayborn Temple in Memphis, TN, Anasa works to build and execute strategies for artists and organizations that are aligned with her vision of a loving world and her belief in creativity as a pathway to personal, community and global transformation.*

www.anasatroutman.com
www.clayborn-temple.org
FB & IG: @anasatoutman
FB & IG: @clayborn_temple

GENESIS 15: 1 – 6

After These Things

Many of us can relate to starting a story by saying something like, "After everything that happened," and much of it has to do with being Black in America. I still feel anger and sadness as I survey the lead crisis in Flint, the third of our men made convicted felons through unfair targeting and sentencing, continuous educational and employment inequities, police brutality, and Boko Haram's capture of the Chibok girls from a school in Nigeria--all in the past five years. All these problems seem to be spawned from the lack of privilege and power to prevent these from happening or to pursue justice when they do. When we say, "after these things," our list is replete with things that have occurred because of lack of access and power. This season of Lent should remind us of the hope of divine provision and promise "after everything that has happened." The challenge with the text is that it centers the promise on a person and not a community, and this is consistent with values that I ascribe to white supremacy, not a loving and just God.

Abram's "After these things" is different because he has rich people's problems and rich people's solutions. In chapter 13, we learn he is heavy with cattle, silver, and gold. He has so much that he and his nephew, Lot, have to part ways because the space they were in was a pond not big enough for fish their size. And, in a white supremacist society, we find that most of our folks are not big fish, but rather we just hope someone among us has two fish and some breads that Love will multiply so that we have enough for the moment. When Lot and company were kidnapped in chapter 14, Abram had trained men on payroll to pursue Lot's captors. We live in a military industrial complex in which the only time Black folks are not antagonized for arming and defending ourselves is when we do it to defend the interests of corporate powers who manipulate politicians to drag us into the military. In the scripture, they offered Abram serious compensation. We come home with PTSD and can still be stopped by racist police officers who do not honor our service or our lives. The GI bill will not offset permanent dysfunction. Yet, after these things, we believe that we have a God who will be a shield for us and either will give us a great reward or be a great reward for us. Is this theology consequential?

I tend to think that what we believe permeates our attitude and actions. Maybe believing that God is a shield prevents our acknowledging the ways that white supremacy has harmed us because doing so may make God's protection seem inadequate. Maybe interpreting the text as God giving Abram an exceedingly great reward hurts us because we see it like trickle-down economics... We believe that trickle-down blessings are sufficient in structured inequity; instead of just distribution, God should bless the powerful in hope of kind distribution to those on the bottom. If we think God will be the great reward, maybe this explains why some use Christianity to cope with state sanctioned violence and the lack of equitable access to the nation's wealth. Trying to identify with Abram can lead to an experience of cognitive dissonance.

While Abram responded in concern for an heir, we are often concerned with providing for our heirs. While Abram had resources galore and "no" child, many of us are afraid to have children because we cannot provide for them. Think of communities of (the working) poor people who send kids to school thankful for free lunch because they struggle to feed their children. Think of the struggle and trauma experienced before saying, "After all the shit I have gone through," before some vision, some word, comes that there is a divine power that will be a shield for us and will reward us for our troubles. The text says God told him to count the stars, if he could, as a metaphor, but what can the number of stars represent for us?

I believe it is the number of ingenuities and sacrifices given by our scholars, elders, and ancestors for our survival. And my hope is that, after these things, we are sustained to be agents to bring about divine Love, Truth, and Justice that resurrects our Black community.

Keith (Sijuwola) Crawford *is an activist and organizer born and formed in Memphis, TN. He studied Jazz Piano Performance, Church Growth at Crichton College. Having served as a music minister for over 20 years, in addition to accepting a call to Christian ministry in 2004, he has since embraced and centered African traditional religion but is passionate about owning all of his experiences and people. In addition to being the owner of Base 10 Mathematics, Siju, as he is called by his friends, has organized with local groups in response to police involved shooting in Memphis, TN, and won labor elections while organizing faculty in K-12 and higher ed. He is currently the Lead Organizer of #UpTheVote901, an org dedicated to seeing more power, information, and representation (PIR) in the hands of more people.*

Third Sunday
in Lent

1 CORINTHIANS 10: 1-13

A Promised Way Out

"No testing has overtaken you that is not common to everyone. God is faithful, and he will not let you be tested beyond your strength, but with the testing he will also provide the way out so that you may be able to endure it." (1 Corinthians 10:13 NRSV)

All of the Bible translations I grew up reading—the ones that were "approved" by the conservative evangelical church I grew up in— translated "testing" in this verse as "temptation," and therefore this passage was almost always applied to sex and used as a key supporting text for what some now call "purity culture."

And while verse eight of this chapter does mention "sexual immorality," it is in the much wider context of talking about the various ways that we are tested and "tempted" and fall short from truly following God. In fact, the very next verse (v14) says, "Therefore, my beloved, flee from idolatry." Not sexuality.

But today, I look back on a passage like this, and my heart is set not on the warning but on the promise: "God is faithful. God *will* provide the way out."

As a white man who is committed to the work of dismantling white supremacy—because I know my liberation is bound up with everyone else's liberation ("I'm not free if you're not free")—I have become more and more aware that to live and move and have my being as a straight white man in this world requires far less endurance than it does for my Black male and female and trans and genderqueer friends and neighbors.

So to be offered a way out so that we can simply endure struggle and oppression may not sound to me like the greatest offer from a Supreme Being, if I'm being honest. Still, what I might take for granted in a scriptural promise like this one is amplified many times over for people of color who are forced to endure suffering from daily microaggressions

—oftentimes by well-meaning white "allies" like me—as well as the burden of systemic racism (policies and systems setup against them) and the ever-present possibility of blatant racist acts perpetrated against them.

To be told that God, the creator of all things, will never allow you to be tested beyond what your strength can bear is essentially to be told that you are infinitely stronger than you realize—and the God of the universe will always have your back.

"Weeping," the psalmist tells us, "may endure for a night, but joy comes in the morning" (Psalm 30:5).

"Love," we are told, "endures all things" (1 Corinthians 13:7).

Strikingly, Jesus said more than once, "Those who endure to the end will be saved" (Matthew 10:22, Matthew 24:13, Mark 13:13).

And that brings us back to 1 Corinthians 10:13 and God's promise to be faithful, to provide the way out, to help us to endure. Yes, we will all be saved. It is for collective liberation that Christ died for us. So when we have done all that we can do, let us stand together. And fight together. And march together.

Forward together, not one step back!

Rev. **Stephen Roach Knight** is national faith organizer for Repairers of the Breach and the Poor People's Campaign: A National Call for Moral Revival. He's also co-founder of Transform Network, a non-profit 501c3 organization dedicated to bringing prophetic voices from the margins to be heard at the center of the body of Christ and to mobilize the whole body of Christ to participate in transformative social action.

Twitter: twitter.com/knightopia
Facebook: facebook.com/knightopia
YouTube: youtube.com/knightopia
Website: transformnetwork.org

ISAIAH 7:10-14

Signs and Shout Outs!

STOP
   No U-Turn
      Exit Ahead
         No Stopping on Highway
            Proceed with Caution
               Speed Limit 60 MPH

Riding down the highway, you can rarely go more than a half a mile without encountering signage directing you towards the nearest gas station, restaurant, or town. The signs are strategically placed to direct us towards our appointed destination.

    MAGA hat wearing students verbally harassing Indigenous people
    Hate-filled speech accompanies a physical attack on Black actor
    Police officer posts racist video of a Black Woman in freezing cold.
    White Nationalists use tiki torches to light up Charlottesville, VA
    Jury offers verdict of "Not Guilty" for cop murder of a Black teen

Rarely, if ever, can you wake up, turn on the news or check the latest news feed on your device without seeing another headline riddled with signs of oppression, racism, hatred, and discrimination warning us of the racist climate we currently live in and foreshadowing what's ahead if we don't initiate the change. Whether we choose to follow the signs or not, they continue to provide us with direction. Regardless of what is happening in the city, state, nation or world, the signs remain.

    In this reading, the prophet Isaiah offers comforting words of instruction and peace in the midst of turmoil. The backdrop of this text is a time of impending war between Judah and Syria. Witnessing the fear emanating from King Ahaz and his people, Isaiah offered words to calm the people and challenge King Ahaz to "Ask Yahweh your God for a sign" (7:11). The Hebrew word for "sign" is 'ôt, which actually has a range of meanings: sign, pledge, token, omen, miracle, and attestation. Signs from God are pledges or promises that something will happen. Unlike threats, they are not intended to alarm; they are simply used as aids to faith, giving support to God's people in times of distress and uncertainty. As proofs, they come in advance of an event, so that when the event takes place, the witnesses might look back and see the sign as a confirmation.

Ahaz's refusal to follow the signs did not stop God from showing them to him, just as refusing to follow highway signs does not stop them from appearing regularly as a part of our journey. As we navigate this life, God repeatedly puts up signs and roadblocks to help direct us. In spite of our human nature to close our eyes or take an alternate path, God continues to redirect us, posting signs on our path and calling us to exercise our faith. Our refusal does not alter God's promises to us.

Human pride may say, "I can do this without any outside help or direction." Can we? Can we experience the freedom so many others want to rob us of? Can we experience the healing so many want to deprive us of? Can we arrive safely at our previously unknown destination without the signs? God has offered us a coupon that cannot be matched – the promise of salvation. Salvation is a free gift from God that comes to us despite our failure to earn it and even despite our previous refusals. Our economic status, nationality, gender or race does not disqualify us from the gift of salvation.

As we look beyond the signs of those who wish to oppress people they deem unworthy, we must focus on God's signs of healing and deliverance. God has promised us forgiveness. God has promised us love. God has promised us peace. God's promises are not limited by the actions of individuals and will not be restricted by hate. God has given us love, salvation, eternal life, and peace.

The sign of the virgin giving birth to a child is the sign for us that our Savior is born. God has promised to birth healing, deliverance, forgiveness, peace and love in our lives. Do not allow the oppressor to cause you to deny the signs of birth!

The angels shouted for all to hear, and we too must shout for all to hear as we drown out the chants and attacks of haters. We stand up and shout out loud: "This is what salvation looks like! An eternal life of God's promises!"

Regina D. Clarke *has Masters degrees in Divinity and Christian Education with an emphasis in Ethics and Social/Restorative Justice from Samuel De-witt Proctor School of Theology at Virginia Union University. She has a heart burst for the Deaf, the Hard of Hearing, the abused, and those who are "for-gotten or discarded" by mainstream society. Her thirst for connecting the community and the church has led her to serve in prisons, domestic violence shelters, and the community-at-large to ensure no person -- despite their past, abilities, or status -- would be denied the opportunity to learn about Jesus and walk faithfully with their God. She currently serves on the ministe-rial staff of Abyssinian Missionary Baptist Church in Memphis.*

PSALM 40:5-10

The Ministry Of Mud Slinging

In an age where the common practice is throwing shade in attempts to gain popularity, social media fans, and reality television contracts, might I suggest that we have mismanaged the mud.

In this rise of empire, power, and privilege it's alarming how many choose to remain stuck in the mud.

Just two weeks ago, after leaving a very powerful worship experience, I came to my car only to find it covered in mud! Apparently, a vehicle that left ahead of me from what appeared to be a grassy parking lot got stuck in mud. Attempting to get loose from their hold, their tires began to sling mud all over the yard. My car just happened to fall prey to the mudslinging taking place on what we have labeled "holy ground." Attempting to not repeat the same process, I took a different route out of the parking lot, only to find myself now stuck in the mud.

Spinning my tires around and around and thinking at any moment this car is going to move now, I discovered after looking in the rearview mirror that I am only slinging mud to the wind. After completely covering my car with another coat of mud, I realized that I'm in too deep.

Like unto David's testimony as it is recorded in Psalm 40, we must wrestle with the notion that we are stuck in this mud hole. Since 2017, our communities have faced hate violence at levels that rival the aftermath of 9/11. People in high places suggest that those who can't get off the ground in this environment must have a personal defect, when the reality is that mud is being slung at them perpetually. The current administration continues to roll out policies that intentionally divide, demean, and demoralize. We are living through a time of spiritual wickedness in high places couched in presidential tweets. We must move from this place of denial (mud-slinging) to a place of liberation for all people.

David skillfully shows us how to survive the mud through persisting in prayer; pursuing power, and peaceful proclamation. We may be stuck in the mud, but we are not stranded. In order to handle the mud you must persist in prayer. Don't lose heart, God is near and pleased to deliver us. Secondly, to navigate the mud we must pursue power. We all must lift our voice and not simply ask the question of what must I do to be saved, but what must we all do to save this nation? We can no longer pray while ignoring the needs of others. After all, the Bible was never intended to be a set of privatized rules but it was given for the liberation, transformation, and reconciliation of all God's children.

David declares that God puts a new song in our mouths and frees us from the burdens of ceremonies and legalism. As we enter this intersection of both justice and mercy, we must sing a new song. Pursue power! Lastly, to handle the ministry of mudslinging we must peacefully proclaim. Let us now move from the despair of selective memory to a place of truth telling. David reminds us to proclaim God's good news without restraint, personally identifying with the Lord and declaring His faithfulness. For far too long, we have privatized our faith while God is calling us to lift our voice! In the words of Hillel the Elder, "If not you, then who, and if not now, then when?"

*Pastor **Hugo Morrison** is a proud alumnus of Regent University, holding a Master's of Divinity Degree in Practical Theology. He serves as the Senior Pastor & Teacher of the Union United Church of Christ, located in Norfolk, Virginia. A great source of strength for Hugo is found in the word of God. In particular, he finds encouragement and renewal in Psalm 27:14, where it states to: "wait on the Lord and be of good courage and He shall strengthen thine heart, wait, I say on the Lord."*

HEBREWS 10: 4-10

It's Not Enough

Let's talk about some things that are impossible: It is impossible to sneeze with your eyes open. It is impossible to drive your car in the air like those futuristic cartoon vehicles on The Jetsons. It is impossible for the Dallas Cowboys to win a Super Bowl (insert evil laugh here). It is impossible for our beloved Aretha or Whitney to come back to life and serenade us with their amazing singing. In the same manner, this writer says that it is impossible for the blood of bulls and goats to take away sins. In other words, the blood that comes from an animal's sacrifice is not enough.

In our world today it seems as if a lot of the tragedy we experience isn't enough. The blood of Black lives which runs in the streets of American cities because police officers have been careless with their guns isn't enough to get strict gun control laws and put these murderous officers in prison for any significant period of time. The countless underage girls who have been brainwashed and battered by R. Kelly aren't enough for society to accept the fact that Black women aren't a priority in a patriarchal society. What will bring change? When will enough be enough? How long will our world stay the same?

The writer says that when Jesus came into the world, he held a conversation with God and laid out God's original intent. God never intended for an animal's sacrifice to be sufficient. God intended for a Savior to come into the world and redeem humankind. It is interesting to me that Jesus is able to tell God what God did not want. I believe that it shows what a divine connection looks like. Jesus was so connected to God that he is able to communicate the will and intent of God to God's people WITHOUT an oppressive framework. Many of our leaders think that they are doing God's will by building border walls, putting children in cages, and making nonviolent offenders serve outrageous prison sentences. This calls their connection into question.

The last verse in our pericope plainly states God's will, for us to be *made* holy. I do not know that we will be made holy in our current context. We commit too many offenses--we lie too much, we steal from one another, and we do not give as we should. We pay women less than men, we allow people to take out loans and adjust the interest rate based on color, we gentrify historic neighborhoods in favor of shopping centers and business parks; however, I do believe that a day is coming when we will be made holy. This is why we strive to be like God, and we hope to one day embody the mission and message of Jesus—because one day we will be made holy. To strive to be like God is to personify the words of the prophet Isaiah, found in the 58th chapter of his book, "...loose the bonds of injustice...undo the thongs of yoke..let the oppressed go free..share your bread with the hungry..bring the homeless poor into your house..cover the naked..do not hide yourself from your own kin." This holiness will be under no efforts of our own, but it will rest upon us because of the body of Jesus-once and for all. I'm grateful that we serve a God who desires for us to take on the form of our Creator. It is my hope that by then, what is not enough will be enough.

Rev. **Jamaar Jones** serves as the Executive Minister at First Baptist Church East End in Newport News, Virginia. He has obtained a Bachelor of Arts degree in English and Foreign Languages from Norfolk State University. He has also obtained a Master of Divinity degree from the Samuel DeWitt Proctor School of Theology at Virginia Union University.

Facebook: Jamaar Jones
Twitter: @_MrJonesSince89
Instagram: jamaarjones

LUKE 13:6-9

Vineyard Chronicles

To the Owners of the Vineyard,

I recently received notice that you gave up on me. Actually, I was informed that you considered me a waste, just using up your soil. To be honest, I was not disappointed by your willingness to give up on me so easily because this type of rejection has become my norm. I had started to embrace rejection, living in this world. Anything counter to it, such as acceptance, compassion and love appeared phony, theatrical and not authentic.

You fail to realize, I have been living in survival mode since the day I arrived at your vineyard.

Seriously, have you surveyed the condition of your vineyard? Who would survive in such conditions? Contrary to what you believe, you have failed at providing a nurturing environment, which would allow reproduction of the fruit you were expecting. Instead, I have experienced years of trauma, neglect and oppression from you—trauma in separation from my family of figs and the firsthand experiences of watching what would befall a fruitless tree. I lived in fear so long, wondering if I would be next, that I programmed my mind to always be ready.

Sadly, every person I grew to love was brutally taken from me. You never considered the impact of the vicarious trauma and its effect on my ability to produce fruit. Instead, you frequently showed up to the vineyard looking only for that which would benefit you and your needs. Your narrow mind restricted you from investigating my environment to research why I was not producing. You valued numbers and celebrated victories without ever exploring the processes to accomplish fruit bearing. You forgot I was a tree in *your* vineyard. You forgot your responsibility to fundamentally establish the necessities for me to blossom fully into my potential. You were so trapped in your wants and desires that you overlooked and neglected the opportunities to be more than just an "owner."

My upbringing raised me to value things and people—value them by properly caring for and nurturing them, loving them, seeing them as equal, and understanding their importance.

Nevertheless, I guess we were raised differently. I mean, you are the owner and I am seen as just a tree, right? Your role as superior--your elevated status—was evident the day I arrived here, so it is no surprise.

Despite your position, you need me as much as I need you.

Now, you are probably waiting for me to apologize for not meeting your expectations, but I will not! I will never apologize for my journey and process. I will never apologize for growing in my own divine and unique way. Instead, I charge you to examine the works of your gardener—you know, the one you employed to care for your vineyard. You apparently forgot how to care for this vineyard after you became an owner; however, this gardener provided hope on days I felt hopeless. My faith increased as the days, week, and years passed away by the mere presence of the gardener. On days I appeared worthless, and felt that way, the gardener continued to care for me and to speak life over me. Even when you wanted to quit on me and felt like I was a waste, the gardener continued to advocate on my behalf, pleading for more time. Do you even know me? Did you take the time to step into the vineyard to touch me, see me, or even speak life in me? No. But the gardener was willing to dig around me, around what you considered mess, and create a new environment to support and nurture growth. The gardener maintained the type of hope that I was more than what appeared, and the gardener watched in anticipation for the day I would produce. I am forever grateful for the gardener!

The next time you are ready to cut us out and get rid of us, adopt the heart and spirit of the gardener. Allow space for your mind and heart to transform, which will allow you to see well beyond the moment, into possibilities. In doing so, your view will be corrected and you too will be able to see: I am not just what I appear to be, but I am what God created me to be.

Sincerely,

The Black & Brown Fig Trees

Minister **Ciarra Smith-Bond** serves as the Young Adult Ministry Leader at Faith Community Baptist Church. She is a wife, mother, probation officer, and community advocate with a calling be a conduit for liberation and rehabilitation. She earned a Bachelor of Science in Criminology and a Master of Divinity from Samuel Dewitt Proctor School of Theology at Virginia Union University.

IG: bottomless_acheiver
Facebook: Ciarra Smith-Bond
Twitter: @godsfav611

1 CORINTHIANS 10:1-4

My Brother Pharaoh

Will Moses mourn the death of Pharaoh, his brother?

This question aims to reframe the role of villain and hero in the Israelite narrative. After all, Moses was a *brother* to the ruler of Egypt. I would imagine that Moses, having grown up as naturalized kin, would have felt something. A broken heart? A disappointment for failing to convince his brethren to act in a way that preserved Egypt from the plagues? Perhaps, he felt the slightest remorse for a sibling who didn't believe the promises proclaimed by God to deliver an oppressed people from captivity by "*many means necessary.*"

Pharaoh had tasted the seduction of power. The idol of power overshadowed a willingness to perceive the truth of the warning from Moses. He ruled with absolute sovereignty over the lives of many people.

Over the span of time, his authority was wielded with exceptional confidence. Unaffected by the woes of suffering people, unpersuaded by proximity to the hardships of slavery, Pharaoh was simply doing what his forefathers had distilled as his divine right in rulership. He had "*Egyptian privilege.*" He lived separate from the ghettos of Goshen. Notwithstanding, racism *certainly* played a role in his society, as it does today with the degradation of God's beloved people. And God loves all people. This means all races, ethnicities, cultures, genders, and creeds.

Will Moses mourn the death of Pharaoh, his brother?

For a time, Pharaoh and Moses walked under the same clouds, lived by the same sea, ate the same food, and drank the same drink. They were bound by familial ties, joined by culture and tradition. Please recall that Moses was at one point a patriotic Egyptian. In light of this, I call each reader to consider the meaning of Pharaoh's death in the life of the Moses. His "brother" died—accosted by the protection of God through sea water. The threat of Hebrew bodily suffering was ended. No more beatings, flogging or bondage. No more senseless killings for being "Hebrew"—a public enemy as indicated by aggression from the governing bodies.

In 1 Corinthians 10:1-3, Paul is reminding the people of Corinth of the dangers of idolatry.

An allegorical device set by the Apostle to help people understand the transient will of humanity to forsake God's protection for the seduction of pride, position, and possession. Thus, carefully consider: Do we endeavor to end racism in service of righteousness and love for God...or for freedom to drink from the same cup as Pharaoh? Let us contemplate the base seduction of our pursuits. If Pharaoh finally passes away, will you mourn the loss of a brother...or...sip from the same cup?

Selah

Lance D. Watson, Jr. *is the eldest son of Pastor Dr. Lance Watson & First Lady Rose Watson. He is the father of two wonderful teens – Kaylee and Lance Watson III. He holds a Bachelors in Business Management/IT Project Management from ECPI University and pursuing a M.Div at the Samuel Dewitt Proctor School of Theology. Lance is a licensed minister, and serves as the Communications Directional Leader for Digital Content at Saint Paul Baptist Church. He proudly serves the Greater Richmond Community as a Brother of Commonwealth Lodge #81 as a Prince Hall Mason in Virginia. He is a lover of books; the Dallas Cowboys – in and out of season; and the Founder of Heirborn LLC – a mentoring fellowship. His ONE WORD is "Legacy."*

Facebook, Instagram, Twitter, and LinkedIn: lancewatsonjr

ISAIAH 55: 1-9

Godness

"The dynamics inherent in the surrender become immediately available to the life of the surrendered person. His life is given back to him at another level. Literally he loses his life and finds it. In the surrender to God in the religious experience, there is no loss of being but rather an irradiation of the self that makes it alive with "Godness". - Dr. Howard Thurman, Creative Encounters

America is at war with its own people. This government has been stripping away basic human rights, and few are exempt. People of Color, LBGTQIA, immigrants, and poor people continue to experience the brunt of America's atrocities and are being pushed further into the margins. In today's climate, it is easy for any oppressed person(s) to forget or even question their own divinity, hopefulness, and worth. Yet in Isaiah 55: 1-9, God clearly reminds us that her ways differ from our own. She (God) also provides salvific hope in *Creative Encounters*, the timeless book by the great mystic, seeker, and theologian, Dr. Howard Thurman: "Religious experience is interpreted to mean the conscious and direct exposure of the individual to God."

God speaks and connects with her children in what Thurman calls creative encounters. These creative encounters will vary and can be experienced through dreams, visions, relationships, phrases, nature, animals, etc. Creative encounters are God's way of demonstrating that she has not forsaken us and that her grace will always be sufficient.

As an interfaith minister, it is important to support others in awakening to how God resonates with their spirits, minds, and hearts. Pierre Teilhard de Chardin once stated, "We are spiritual beings having a human experience." In my ministry, I teach that God is present and available where you are. How important it is to commune with God in the most natural way to you! Wherever your passion lies, I can assure you that God speaks to and through you in that medium. For example, if you like to dance, you are praying with your body. Are you a singer? Your singing is an instrument for God. Do you enjoy music? Your melody is creating God's sound to be felt in your spirit and the spirit of others.

When I share these simple truths, people that I serve began to make a connection to how God is present within their everyday lives. Dr. Thurman shared that Eckhart insists "that there is in the soul of man, an apex, a spark which is God, the God-head. The God-head is the very ground of the soul." Our God-head is fed through prayer, meditation, contemplation, reflection, and action. These methods could be utilized to cultivate your relationship with God. Personally, I have experienced some of the most insightful creative encounters through prayers, chants, and singing. Creative encounters are moments where growth is inevitable, if we choose what God has brought to and for our betterment.

Keyona Saquile Lazenby is the founder of Blessed is She, an interfaith women's ministry that provides services and offerings to help women achieve self-actualization. Keyona is passionate about delivering pre and post-release services to system-involved populations. She is an adjunct professor with the Prison University Project/Patten University. An avid traveler, she believes that cultural exploration is the world's greatest teacher. She received her Master's in Social Transformation and Certificate of Women Studies in Religion from Pacific School of Religion/Graduate Theological Union. She is currently pursuing a Certificate of Advanced Professional Studies at Pacific School of Religion and plans to enter a Ph.D. program in the Fall of 2020. Rev. Keyona is an ordained interfaith minister and a graduate of One Spirit Interfaith Seminary.

Website: www.blessedis.org

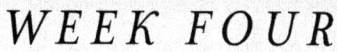

Fourth Sunday
in Lent

2 CORINTHIANS 5:16-21

White Protestant Reconciliation is Genocide

All hail the great white protestant idol of reconciliation.

Bow before its ivory towers and its endless chants for justice—justice defined by its high priest "wokeness" who has been birthed from the perfect progressive seminary. Who has read everything Dr. James Cone wrote but still thinks Reinhold Niebuhr makes some great points, and we shouldn't just discard the latter. This high priest sees the value of your dead children; they make perfect hashtags for their twitter profile. Yes, Yes, the High Priest of white reconciliation has Black acolytes. He always keeps a few tied up in the back in case you ask and will post pictures with them at the oh-so-opportune time.

Come follow the mainline contingent as we go to bow before reconciliation. We will sacrifice repentance and reparations on the altar of reconciliation. For the idol demands Black blood and assimilation. Sing the hymn the way we teach you to sing and say the words of white lament the way we want you to, little Black boy. We call you that because we demanded your manhood so long ago. Yes, we want you to come tell us about racism and how broken we are. Do all the emotional labor for us so we can go back to the yearlong liturgy of not giving two cares about you.

What you have just read is the prayer of white protestant reconciliation. It is the secret prayer of white church and, at times, the church writ large. If what Paul says is true, and everything old passes away, then what can be older and more broken than white supremacy? What could have a more scarred visage on the face of a nation then this mask of civility that is actually empire? What could be in more need of resurrection? What Paul is discussing is not the weak ineffectual attempts at apologies and singing "kumbaya" that often is passed off as racial justice in this country. He is talking about the total and complete dismantling of the entire empire. For in a new creation, the world as we know it is facing itself in the mirror and sees how full of emptiness and want it is. How in need it is to be deconstructed and rebuilt as the Kin-dom of God.

Your reconciliation is a joke. If you aren't committing to divest from whiteness and return what you stole from my ancestors and me, how dare you call yourself an Ambassador to Christ? How can you be an Ambassador to a reality so foreign, so otherworldly, so antithetical to this world that when it came to love us, we lynched it and hung it from a tree? *You lynch still.* The truth is you don't want justice, you want passivity. The truth is you don't want true reconciliation, you want me to bury your sins in the cotton fields where you buried my great great grandma. You want me to get on my knees this Maundy Thursday and wipe the blood from your hands and make sure I clean your feet from the sweat of my siblings' backs that you walked on to get over here. You want me to sell you hope from a pauper's position because you haven't left me anything to live on. You want me as a called and ordained minister of the church of Christ to offer you absolution. To loose you here so you will be loosed in heaven.

I won't.

For far too long now you have come to me hoping that I will let reconciliation slip through my hands and into your hungry starved mouth. What you think is a full belly is an illusion, and what you have drunk from isn't living water but the very sands of the desert of your own exile. For far too long, you thought the gilded cage of white supremacy was comfortable.

Lay in your bed. You made it.

I leave you this Lent to your God. I hope that same God offers you the same mercy you granted me a-la the Lord's Prayer. Amen.

Lenny Duncan *(he/him/his) is a follower of Jesus Christ and is in a passionate love affair with Grace. He is the Pastor of Jehu's Table, a church of justice, radical welcome, and a place where "all" means all. He is also a frequent voice on the intersection of the Church and the cries of the oppressed. He pays special attention to Black liberation movements in his work, but lifts up the intersection with other marginalized peoples. He believes that the ELCA has remained so white because of a theological problem, not a sociological one. He holds a Master of Divinity from United Lutheran Seminary. His book* Dear Church: A Love Letter from a Black Preacher to the Whitest Denomination in the U.S *from Fortress Press is available for pre-order on most major book retailers and is set for release July 2, 2019.*

2 CORINTHIANS 5: 16-21

Continually New

Once I heard a nun speak, and as part of her introduction she told us about her order's charism—the particular gift her group brings to the body of Christ. "We devote our lives to repentance," she said. I'm not sure if everyone in the room was as skeptical as I was, but she continued: "These days we like to call it continual conversion."

This seemed to me a radical bit of theology. To imagine repentance, not as a sackcloth-and-ashes performance, but as a constant re-turning to God; an attitude of humility, of always looking to learn and re-learn love and faith. Repentance: in the original Greek, turning—something we must continually do, not because we are inherently evil, but because life is hard, the world lies, and God is always inviting us to better.

The most difficult conversion is always to turn away from the god of my own false selves. Whether it's a layer of pretense I've carefully constructed, or a way of being I almost feel that I was born with—no matter how destructive it reveals itself to be, letting go of my ego feels like danger, and often like grief. For a long time, then, there is an in-between: the terror and exhilaration of letting go, over and over, letting the true self upend everything—and of letting anyone, anyplace catch a glimpse of that long-hidden self, frail and unwieldy and beautiful.

Then one day, there is peace, and the realization that at some point in the night, the old has gone, the new has come.

As a white person living in a white supremacist world, I have come to cling to the idea of continual conversion. It reminds me that when it comes to dismantling white supremacy, I will always be returning to the basics, learning from and striving to be accountable to the marginalized. It allows me to move beyond shame, into repentance and action, when I discover I've made yet another mistake.

And this process has invited me into a truer self. Many of us are familiar with the idea of converting from a false self to a true one on an individual level, but this is also what we do when we repent from whiteness (or internalized racism) in the context of our families, neighborhoods, or society.

When I recognize defensiveness or fragility in myself, it's a sign that I am overidentified with whiteness—an invitation to loosen my grip and see what emerges when I listen to Spirit, follow, and wait. When my friends of color struggle against self-hatred, or when any of us face temptation to defend systems of power and privilege that benefit us, there is the possibility of getting stuck in a quagmire of anger or shame.

But there is also the possibility to be made new. To set aside a false self, false power, false love, or false progress and have the courage to seek truth. To turn away from dominant culture and racist systems that seek to determine our identity or value; and to turn instead toward the voice of God speaking our true name, the hands of God still shaping our true selves, the arms of God reaching to welcome and reconcile us again and again to God, the world to the world—and even ourselves to ourselves.

Lyndsey Medford *is an indecorous Southerner, an erstwhile evangelical, and an inexpert advocate for justice. She is Director of Discipleship at Two Rivers UMC, a new church start in Charleston, SC, that aspires to be radically inclusive, anti-racist, and creative. She writes regularly about creativity, Jesus, justice, and bodies on Instagram and at lyndseymedford.com.*

JOSHUA 5:12

The Day The Manna Stopped

"The manna stopped the day after they ate this food from the land; there was no longer any manna for the Israelites, but that year they ate the produce of Canaan." (Joshua 5:12)

"Look into soggy blue eyes with love for the poor
Sickly, tired, toothless beast
Kill him for his own good, roll his head with love
If you cannot hate
But roll his head
Disrupt, disrupt
Everything that disturbs you
Throw lit cigarettes in trash cans, turn underground
Cattle cars into terror and even death machines
Put tense filled hands to use, Disrupt!"
—Kuwasi Balogon, from the poem, "If You Love Them, Wouldn't You Like to See Them Better Off?"

"This is a new day; we don't sing those words any more. In fact, the whole song should be discarded. Not 'We Shall Overcome,' but 'We Shall Overrun.'"
—Martin Luther King, Jr. in *Where Do We Go From Here: Chaos or Community*

What do those who have been part of the movement do when the movement moves on? When those we have been fighting alongside take the fight in a different direction? When the communities we advocate for start advocating for themselves? When young activists insist on abandoning both the faith-based structures and the faith-based leaders of past fights in favor of a new approach? What do we do when a new generation no longer wants to sit with us at the campfire singing "Kumbaya" but takes to the street to "throw lit cigarettes into trash cans, turn underground cattle cars into terror and even death machines? Put tense filled hands to use" and "Disrupt" not only systems of injustice but the very fabric of the movement itself? What do we do when they insist on singing "We Will Overrun" instead of "We Shall Overcome?"

Movements always have an end to which they are moving and often have to change directions mid-march to reach this preferred end. Rebellions and revolutions require a clear, ultimate objective, but tactics and strategies change as new leaders take to the fight and as opponents change their own strategy and objectives. The problem that many movement leaders have is that we are ultimately more drawn to the fight than we are to the outcomes. Once the fight shifts and we are seen as either a detriment to the movement or completely obsolete, we tend to react with emotions ranging from anger, to mourning, to disdain.

The story in Joshua 5:9-12 is instructive. God has liberated the Israelites from slavery in Egypt, led them through the desert, and delivered them to the promised land. Once there, the people paused to celebrate God's past act in the Passover and then they harvested food from the land. The text editorializes at this point: "The manna stopped the day after they ate this food from the land." This represents a profound change in the Israelites' daily relationship with God.

Viewed from God's perspective, this must have been an agonizing moment. Having sent Moses to liberate the Israelites from Egypt, mothered them through the wilderness, provided their every need, suddenly God is not needed in the same way. Under the leadership of a young man, and freshly delivered into the promised land, the Israelites feed themselves and begin the business of establishing self-sufficient lives in a new land. God knew how many mistakes they would make, how difficult the relationship would become, and yet…. Yes, and yet, God stepped back, stopped the manna, and allowed the people to care for themselves. God in God's wisdom understands something we often miss. For God the exodus is not just about the act of liberation but the creation of a liberated people. It is not just the journey from Egypt, through the desert, to the promised land that was important so much as that very first meal Joshua and his people prepared and ate for themselves, that first manna-less day. It was that first moment of liberated self-sufficiency that was the point of all that went before.

During this season of Lent many of us need to ask ourselves: "Are we force feeding our communities manna when we should be stepping back and celebrating how well they are feeding themselves?" And many of us need to understand that sometimes the best act of liberative practice is stepping aside to let others lead.

*Rev. Dr. **Joseph W. Caldwell** serves as the President of the Memphis Center for Urban Theological Studies in Memphis, TN. MCUTS is a regionally accredited institution of higher education serving lower income students with limited educational options. Dr. Caldwell has also served as a Chaplain, Pastor, and Professor. His work evolves around awakening white churches to the realities of white abuses of power. He is currently working on a theology of power and privilege in conversation with James Cone and is also writing a series of personal essays tentatively entitled* Whitey Got Woke: Sort Of. *He also wishes someone cooler had taken his bio pic.*

JOSHUA 5: 9-12

Egyptian Ex-Pat in the Promised Land

I come to this writing humbled. I've been sitting here with all my self-righteous, social-justice-y thoughts about the book of Joshua, the Exodus, the problematic colonization of the Promised Land...and...I'm humbled.

Whenever I try to apply scripture to my life, I first have to ask myself where I am positioned vis-a-vis the people in the text. As a white, documented American citizen, I am certainly not positioned as a Hebrew refugee who escaped from slavery in Egypt and is just now setting foot, in this passage, into the Promised Land. That means I don't get to offer commentary from that place.

So who am I? The best I can discern, I am an Egyptian sympathizer with the Hebrew people and a kind of stowaway on the great Hebrew freedom train. I am a would-be defector from the oppressor culture in which I am still granted most of the privileges of citizenship. Exodus 12 tells us that "many other people" went with the Hebrew slaves on their midnight journey out of Egypt (Exodus 12: 38). I long to be in that number! But I recognize that I am not fully trustworthy as a fellow traveler. I have Egyptian connections. If my feet start to hurt or I have a disagreement with the Hebrew leadership, I can turn back to the land of oppression, and, in so doing, potentially betray the whereabouts of the escapees whose lives are on the line. What's more, having been socialized into oppressor culture, I carry it with me in my expectations, my mannerisms, my internalized feeling of superiority of which I may or may not be conscious. I may, unconsciously, try to keep the Hebrew travelers "in their place." I may have designs on leadership, consciously or unconsciously, even though I would inevitably just end up steering us back to Egypt or another place like it, since that's what would feel like home to me. (I wonder if it was the Egyptian co-travelers who came up with the idea of slaughtering all the Canaanites in the Promised Land, well-versed as they were in the ways of empire.)

I am so curious about those Egyptians who joined the Exodus. I am sure they had their reasons. Maybe, like me, they were queer—ill-fitted to the gender roles sanctioned by the dominant Egyptian culture or the romantic proclivities that were considered "moral" within it. Maybe they were working class Egyptians who recognized that they too were being exploited to enrich Pharaoh and his ilk. There are many reasons why they might have wanted to get out, but they still were not Hebrews, and they most likely would not have known their type of suffering.

To be allowed to come along….This is simply a grace gift—from God, yes, but also from the Hebrew people who had no reason to trust them (us). I feel this so deeply—when I remember to!—that my friendships with people of color, and especially with the Black and Indigenous people alongside whom I struggle against white supremacy, are grace gifts of which I can never be deserving. I am humbled. I am so grateful.

And especially so because this story has a bitter punchline: We are not yet in the Promised Land, we who live in the United States in 2019. We are still in Egypt, and our Hebrew loved ones are still at risk every moment of being brutalized or worse. But I hear the Freedom Train coming. I know some of the people who are organizing it. And so, what am I doing to prepare the way for it? What are we doing—we who are white and long for Exodus—to provision people of color for the journey on which we need them to lead us? What resources are we able to expropriate from our Egyptian families, employers, institutions, and community members? How can we decolonize our own spirits? Are we ready for the long wilderness time when we will feel awkward and uncomfortable all the time, unfamiliar with being followers of someone else's leadership? How much are we willing to risk and release to make way for the freedom journey?

Nichola Torbett *is a spiritual seeker, recovering addict, gospel preacher, podcaster, writer, resistance fomenter, dog-walker, nonviolent direct action trainer, and aspiring race traitor. Driven by her passion for both spiritual formation and social change, she co-founded* Seminary of the Street, *a training academy for love warriors, in 2009 and Second Acts, a liturgical direct action affinity group, in 2014. She is co-editor of* Resipiscence: a Lenten Devotional for Dismantling White Supremacy *and a contributor to* The Word Is Resistance, *a podcast from SURJ-Faith and SURJ-Action, as well as to Jesus Radicals, The Yoke, and other radical discipleship publications. She likes to lock herself to things at strategic moments.*

Facebook: Nichola Torbett
Blog: https://thelongingisthecompass.wordpress.com

PSALM 32

The Pain of a Shameful System

Meek Mill was being interviewed on CNN about his song with Jay Z entitled "What's Free?" and his and Jay's initiative for criminal justice reform. The reporter asked him if he was the right person to speak on criminal justice reform since he'd been in jail. Meek Mill could barely contain himself when he said, "I've always wanted to be on CNN to speak for the countless voices that can't speak for themselves. I've been in the criminal justice system since I was 18. I got arrested because I was suspended from school, and instead of telling my single mother that her son got suspended, I tried to go back to school. They arrested me for trespassing. Then I got another charge for a narcotics agent busting in a house, and they said I pointed a gun at three officers. Let me ask you a question. Do you think a young Black man in Philly could point a gun at three officers with guns in their hands and live to tell about it? I used to be ashamed that I had a record because I didn't value my own story, but not anymore, because there is a system that tries to keep us in shame."

The psalmist proclaimed, "Oh what joy for those whose disobedience is forgiven, whose sin is put out of sight! Yes, what joy for those whose record the lord has cleared of guilt, whose lives are lived in complete honesty! When I refused to confess my sin, my body wasted away, and I groaned all day long."

How many young Black men and women are groaning in jails and prisons with shame from being caught up in a system that silences their pain? Meek Mill had to acknowledge the shame but also identify the sickness in a racist structure that seeks to silence the survivors of poverty and urban city life. What pain are young Black men and women in urban cities holding in? The prophet Marvin Gaye proclaimed a long time ago, "It makes me want to holler the way they do my life." But when these young people are not given the medium to express and expose the injustice, their bones waste away. They don't fully know their value.

The only relief for our young people who are wasting away in these modern day plantations is for them to cry out to a God of justice: "Therefore, let all the godly pray to you while there is still time, that they may not drown in the floodwaters of judgment." It was a Black female judge that put Meek Mill back in jail for violating his probation. The reporter tried to discount Meek's claim that the criminal justice system is corrupted by structural racism because a Black judge put him away. Meek alluded that even a Black judge is not exempt from the corruption of unconfessed pain that turns into self-hatred.

Many young Black people are both spiritually and physically locked up before they stand before earthly judges. They have never been able to confess their shame as they drown in the floodwaters of judgment. But when they confess to God their value, God is the one that releases them from the spiritual prison of self-condemnation. Therefore "there is now no condemnation for those that are in Christ Jesus!"

Jesus knew what it was like to be unjustly condemned, betrayed by his own people, and caught up in a system of Roman oppression. Jesus had a chance to be released by Pontius Pilate and was told to confess or speak up concerning his charges:

and he went back into the Praetorium. "Where are You from?" he asked. But Jesus gave no answer. So Pilate said to Him, "Do You refuse to speak to me? Do You not know that I have authority to release You and authority to crucify You?" Jesus answered, "You would have no authority over Me if it were not given to you from above. Therefore the one who handed Me over to you is guilty of greater sin."…

The greater sin is when we hold people captive that are really the victims of a corrupt system. Jesus became the scapegoat for all that was corrupt so that those who would follow might be set free. If we confess our sins to God, our shame, our dysfunction, our pain, he is faithful to forgive. We don't have to hold it in anymore, for Jesus has come to set the captives free.

Dr. **Stacy L. Spencer** is the Senior Pastor of New Direction Christian Church in Memphis, Tennessee. Dr. Spencer's Kingdom mindset led to the development of Eden Square Town Center, a community model intended to reinvigorate a Memphis food desert. Dr. Spencer is the author of 3D Relationships: Three Relationship Dimensions to Lead You Into Your Purpose and U-Turn: A 12 Step Guide to Spiritual Transformation. He is chairman of the board for Power Center Community Development Corporation. Dr. Spencer earned a Doctorate of Divinity from Drew University, a Masters of Divinity from Southern Baptist Theological Seminary and a Bachelors from Western Kentucky University He and Rhonda Spencer are the proud parents of four sons, Calvin, Omari, Jordan and Jaden.

LUKE 15:1-3, 11B-32

Actions Speak As Loudly As Words

"Now all the tax collectors and sinners were coming near to listen to him. And the Pharisees and the scribes were grumbling and saying, "this fellow welcomes sinners and eats with them." So he told them this parable" Luke 15:1-3

Ancient society was rooted in economic and social discrimination, roots that still run deep today. There was a great divide in the Roman world between the haves and the "have nots." In his book *From Shame to Self-Worth*, Edward Wimberly describes this ancient society as a "class stratified system where a person's worth was value-laden based on honor and shame." The honor/shame system explains the resistance that Jesus encounters from the Pharisees and scribes in this Lukan narrative. They complain and grumble about Jesus' association with unscrupulous government employees and sinners. Not only does Jesus associate with tax collectors and sinners, but Jesus has the audacity to break the rules of ritual purity and eat with the social outcasts of his day. So in their critique of Jesus actions, they ignore his outreach and paint him as a not-so-secret sympathizer with sinners: "This fellow welcomes sinners and eats with them."

The Pharisees and Scribes were the product of the world in which they lived--a world ordered by boundaries where shame and honor were pivotal values. Not unlike the Pharisees and scribes, we too live in a world that assigns value to people according to social hierarchies. Women, children, people of color, and persons with disabilities are often seen as less important than others. Senior citizens, the poor, the working poor, persons who struggle with mental illness, the homeless, LGBT+, and other marginalized individuals are not always looked upon with honor but are often overlooked or disdained. It is the same ordering of value based social hierarchies that has resulted in a flourishing of oppressive ideologies that sanction racism, sexism, homophobia, classism, ageism, and xenophobia which seek to suppress the liberation of others. In fact, in the current climate minority groups are often the target of venomous rhetoric that uses coded language to justify hate crimes as patriotism, white supremacy as heritage, and racial profiling as security. Many children are coming of age in a culture that, despite the Voting Rights Act, the Civil Rights Act, Brown vs Board of Education and other landmark legislation, still places value upon the very arbitrary human distinctions that Martin Luther King, Jr., Ella Baker, Diane Nash, the Civil Rights Movement, SNCC, Rainbow PUSH, the NAACP and other advocates and advocacy agencies have worked so tirelessly to dismantle.

Jesus' actions demand space for reflection in this narrative because simply in sharing a meal with sinners and tax collectors, Jesus upset the hierarchical structure of his time with what were deemed socially disruptive and offensive actions. Jesus challenged the boundaries, removed the limits, and rejected the social assumptions which shaped and guided the people of his day.

So, in response to the inquiry of the scribes and Pharisees, Jesus tells them a parable to show why he eats with tax collectors and sinners. In this parable about a lost sheep, a lost coin, and a lost son, he invites the religious authorities to reject the categories which limit and devalue human life and relationships and embrace a vision that embodies the values of the kingdom of God--a kingdom that challenges the prevailing social order and creates tables where all are welcome to live free and empowered. Jesus' actions are contrarian in that they call for a response that is contrary to the prevailing norms. He reverses the established order by his actions of inclusivity. For Jesus, actions speak as loudly as words.

The season of Lent beckons us to live each day by reassigning value to those which have been devalued and limited by categories, oppressive ideologies, and theologies. The love of God frees us from the insidiousness of social hierarchies and double standards which often do nothing more than hurt or limit others. Jesus invites us to go and do likewise by embodying a presence that welcome others to feast at the table not just of Christ, but with Christ.

*Rev. Dr. **Gina Marcia Stewart** is a pastor, visionary, preacher, and builder. She has served as the Senior Pastor of Christ Missionary Baptist Church since March 1995. She currently serves as the 1st-Vice President of Lott Carey Foreign Missions Convention and is a member of the National Board of the NAACP. She is a Visiting Professor of Practical Theology for the Samuel D. Proctor School of Theology at Virginia Union University.*

IG-DrGinaMStewart
FB Personal-Gina M. Stewart
FB Public-Dr. Gina M. Stewart
Twitter-@drgmstewart

JOSHUA 5:9-12

We Bore The Shame

We bore the shame.
People saved from famine
Saved from a chosen one of our own
To become strangers in a land that was ours
The knowledge of our role, the land's salvation and survival unknown

We bore the shame of becoming slaves in a land we once called home;
Far from a land of promise yet for generations shackled to the bone.
A nomadic people used to movement no longer able to move free;
Subject to the might and rule of the great Egyptian Pharoah's dynasty.

Yet through the power of God's mighty hand,
A people now move toward its promised land.
The reproach of Egypt has now been taken away;
Erecting an altar unto God with the tribes' 12 stones at Gilgal that selfsame day.
Keeping the Passover as the Lord commanded, unleavened cakes and parched corn on the morrow they did eat.
For the manna that provided from heaven in the wilderness had now ceased.
For they had come to the land of promise and ate the fruit of the land that year
No threat of famine or spoil; there was nothing to fear.

Unlike the people of Israel whose reproach was rolled away,
The African American still suffers the stigma and with great pain.
The cries for freedom and the blood of countless sisters and brothers yet cry from the ground.

We've sung, marched, cried, demanded freedom yet as an echo those sounds abound.

How shall we remove the reproach?
How shall we remove the stain?
When media constantly perpetuates stereotypes
And we're continually looked upon with disdain.

How shall we remove the reproach?
How shall we remove the stain?
Yet still fighting over voting rights and equal treatment under the law;
ain't a damn thing changed.

How shall we remove the reproach?
How shall we remove the stain?
When new developments push me out of my own community;
where I was born and raised?
Neighbors are now a Starbucks and those who want to question my identity again.

The ancestors who survived the middle passage;
The ancestors who survived the chains;
The ancestors who fled carried a message;
We were all born free, never a slave.

So this selfsame day we acknowledge the only one who could remove such reproach.
It will take more than legislation, more than a congressional vote.
It will take the one who brought through the wilderness his children to the place of Gilgal.
Here in America, we will arise from the mountain peaks to the desert plains to recall our deliverance within this land.
We will set our individual and corporate prayers as a memorial before the Lord,
For the manna has long since ceased and we will fight, build and work to get the fruit of the land our ancestors worked for.

Monica Leak *is the editor and a contributing writer of,* Faith of our Founders 100 Daily Devotionals to Inspire, Encourage and Propel the Finer Woman. *She contributed writings for* The Road to Calvary: Surviving a Season of Suffering, *a Lenten devotional and to* Resipiscence: A Lenten Devotional for Dismantling White Supremacy. *She is a school based speech-language pathologist in Maryland, a librarian for the John Leland Center for Theological Studies where she is also a student and an associate minister at First Baptist Church Vienna.*

Monica Leak on Instagram and Facebook
MoPrayer on Twitter

Fifth Sunday
in Lent

ISAIAH 43:16-21

Lord, It's Hard to Watch You Die

When Jesus got to the place of his execution, he was placed on his back with arms outstretched. The nails were first driven through small wooden disks to eliminate any chance of the heads pulling through the flesh. The site of the incision in the arm was critical; the Romans perfected the procedure. The legionnaire given the task felt for a specific spot; the nail would be driven between the bones of the forearm close to the wrist while not severing any major arteries or veins. There is a space between eight small bones which is structurally suitable to permit a full body weight to be supported. If the nails had been driven into the palms of the hands, under the extreme weight, they would have ripped out between the fingers.

First, a nail would have been driven into his arm on one side, and then the other. The legionnaire would make sure that his arms were not pulled too tightly, allowing flexion and movement. With this done, the crossbar was then raised and affixed to the stripe. The next stage involved the nailing of the feet, also deliberately. The third nail had to be driven through both feet, which were turned outward so the nail could be hammered inside the Achilles tendon. With his knees slightly flexed, Jesus was now crucified. As he slowly sagged down, he would have tried to support his weight with the muscles of his legs, an impossible position to maintain. In some cases, the victims' legs were broken, so they couldn't support themselves in this way. Eventually more and more weight was placed upon the nails.

The Romans ensured that crucifixion would create fear in those who opposed and wanted to rise up against the empire. Public hangings were meant to silence any uprisings. Families of the victims would watch in horror as their loved ones hung painfully until their diaphragms went into spasm and they suffocated to death.

The graphic detailed description of Jesus being put to death causes me to feel as if I should just give up hope.

"let me fall, let me fall, it's not worth it anymore"
"Hard to Watch Me Die," Tracy Howe Wispelway

Prophetic witnesses remind us through poetry and song that our daily experiences of loss and trauma with white supremacy are linked to our bodies and our spirituality. Wispelway's words haunt me because I envision Christ watching his body through the bodies of innocent African-descended people. Their blood is Jesus' blood. Some of the deaths are committed by state-sanctioned violence. Jesus was sentenced to die by the Roman Empire—state sanctioned violence.

Tamir Rice, Trayvon Martin, Michael Brown, Sandra Bland, Eric Garner, Rekia Boyd, Philando Castille, Charleena Lyles, LaQuan McDonald, Botham Shem Jean, Oscar Grant, Emanic Fitzgerald Bradford, Jr., Mya Hall, Jordan Edwards, Aiyana Stanley Jones,and Jemel Robinson, Maurice Stallard, and Vicki Lee Jones

My heart hurts when hatred and overt racism motivates these murders.

"Don't think for a moment I never felt the pain. You can't imagine the hurt and the shame. They put the nails through my hands, pierced my side, please understand, it wasn't easy, but it was worth it."
"It Wasn't Easy," CeCe Winans

Lord, it's hard to watch you die over and over again. Such moments send me running to the scriptures to look for hope among oppressed people in ancient times. Looking for a word from them to encourage my soul, like the prophets, especially Isaiah. 43:16-21 brings me some peace: "Be alert, be present; I'm about to do something brand new. It's bursting out! Don't you see it? There it is! I'm making a road through the desert, rivers in the badlands" (The Message).

Is there hope during this Lenten season? Yes, I remain hopeful because the myths of white skin supremacy are false and cannot win. I believe God is doing a new thing in 2019. I hear God calling us by name and empowering us to dismantle and eradicate systems of oppression and tyranny. I know God is speaking life into a new generation of prophetic leaders across this nation to call out Legion and say the names of powers and principalities enacting evil upon innocent people. For now, the angry white supremacist mob continues to shout "Crucify

Black and Brown bodies! Crucify those who do not bow down to white supremacy! Crucify them!"

I know the myth of white skin superiority will die. The myth of a dominant culture must die. The myth of a dominant race must die. And internalized oppression as a result of the myths must die.

Velda Love *serves as Minister for Racial Justice in The Justice and Local Church Ministries of The United Church of Christ National Office in Cleveland, OH. The goal of her work is to dismantle and eradicate racism by understanding the role and intent of the creation of colorism categories, the construction of whiteness , and people of color myths. Velda brings an African-centered, black liberation, and Womanist approach to the Bible and theology, placing God at the center of life and faith.*

Facebook VRaye Love
Instagram vrayelove (The Rev. Dr. Love)
Twitter @vrayelove

ISAIAH 43: 16-21

Tender and Resilient

To be the hands, feet and heart of God
Requires you to close your eyes, take a deep, slow breath,
And open your eyes again, but wait!
You have to open them like you are waking up from a 100-year nap
You have to open them like you've been asleep all this time and now you
are coming to
And everything is brand new
You truly haven't seen anything like this before!
You have to look around with a wide-eyed wonder
As all the chatter of your dreams and strivings
The cacophony and the chaos and the nonsense, everything you think
you know, and
Everything you think each thing is
Falls silent in the newness of being really awake

To be the hands, feet and heart of God
You have to act like
The world was handed to you fresh today
And you had amnesia about despair and bitterness and dread
You forgot to expect disappointment and to anticipate failure
Yes, you have to be that foolish! The exact thing you were taught
You better not be
New and hopeful and expectant
And as tender and innocent
As the green shoot that insists on weaving its tendrils
Around cement
And so God lives

Soo Hyun Han-Harris *is an educator and fighter for quality public education in Oakland, which she has called home for more than 25 years. She
is blessed to have been part of First Congregational Church of Oakland
since 2003, ever since she felt the spirit of real, just and conscious relation-
ship-building and change-making in the community. As a lover of people
and a new mother, her deepest wish is to see Oakland be the diverse,
equitable and life-giving community that Jesus worked to build.*

Facebook: Soo Hyun Han

JOHN 12:1-8

Economies of Anointing

The chief priests and Pharisees had just sent out an order: anyone who knew where Jesus was must report it so that they could arrest him. Caiaphas, the high priest that year, said it was better for one to die for the People rather than the whole nation be destroyed.

This was right before the Passover, right before the People would come together, from all over, to remember their collective liberation from slavery. This was right before Jesus would enter Jerusalem, as the center of a mobilization, publicly defiant, and countering Rome's triumphal entry.

In the middle of these events, Mary anoints Jesus. A healing act, an intimate and, perhaps even an erotic moment between the two. Anointing his feet with her hair. Her hair and his feet drenched in nearly one pound of "costly perfume made of pure nard." He knew he was heading toward the end. She, reading the signs of the times, also knew and may have known what was on his human heart, that he needed a moment of care, to experience love manifested physically before his body entered the time of torture. The air in the room filled with the aroma of the perfume before the air in the city filled with the smell of blood, sweat, and vinegar. He needed a moment of solidarity – to be truly seen, if even for a moment, by someone outside of his own body, by someone who knew the struggles of their People, and by someone who understood what was to come. She knew both his power and his vulnerability. Mary was a healing presence. *She* anointed the Anointed One.

To be a healing presence, one has to open themselves up, connecting to the wounds of another. Intimate. Both allow themselves to be vulnerable, dropping walls; both are willing to listen in a different way, to learn, and to adapt. They are willing to give and receive whatever is mutually healing in the moment.

Whenever I think of this moment, I wonder who has access to such healing presence today?

Who do we prioritize when we give our healing love, fully and healthily?

Brown and Black bodies experience oppression of their bodies, minds, and hearts everyday and for generations and generations. Has our healing been prioritized?

Have our historical wounds and generational trauma made it hard for us to know how to give and receive those things that will heal us?

Dismantling white supremacy means taking inventory of those to whom we give our healing selves. Those who have less access, who tend to be isolated and selected out, whom Empire has deemed to be less worthy— queer, trans, POC, immigrant, disabled, historically colonized, working class? Do we ensure that modes of love, care, healing, and solidarity are given to us/them and are accessible? Or do we reserve them for those who have certain amounts of privilege and access, so we don't have to bear as much responsibility or so that we don't accidentally catch a glimpse of our wounded selves?

While it is true that we cannot choose who we fall for, we can choose who we actively love, who we prioritize, and who we connect with intimately and give our friendship and solidarity to.

Will we allow ourselves to be anointed by the People, to be immersed in their experiences, struggles, and wounds, and allow them to be immersed in ours, or will we continue to give our resources and ourselves in ways we always have? In ways that are comfortable? In ways that help *ourselves* get ahead?

Will we continue to surround ourselves by the same folks we have always surrounded ourselves with? Are we daring enough to look into the hearts of the Other and allow them to look into ours?

Jesus says, "You always have the poor with you, but you do not always have me."

He is right. We will always have the *empowered* poor and oppressed. And we/they need more than the 300 denarii. We/They need our presence. We/They need us to show up. And we/they are the ones who anoint us, preparing the way for liberation to enter into this world when we/they tend to our collective wounds.

May we be intentional, strategic, and discerning with our healing presence and healing hearts.

*Rev. **Jeanelle Nicolas Ablola** is a second-generation Filipino American, queer, trans, neurodivergent, anti-imperialist, and is currently serving at Pine UMC, San Francisco. They are rooted in the movement for national democracy in the Philippines and regularly lead solidarity trips to the country. They are Co-Chair of the UMC Cal-Nev Philippine Solidarity Task Force (PSTF) and a member of the National Ecumenical-Interfaith Forum for Filipino Concerns - NorCal (NEFFCON). They serve Christ through serving the People.*

YouTube - https://www.youtube.com/channel/UChrHe2ED-QIG9wx3TfB7Ncw

ISAIAH 43:16–21

Perception

a child's footprints through the desert that end miles from a place to
call home;
parched from religions that don't quench and faucets that murder;
unnamed bloated bodies float to the surface.

new, new, new;
new beach-front property as if to know wilderness.
shame, heritage, and certainty as blistering as the sand
bind to the former things.

God is doing a new, new, new thing...
Resonance springs forth like a healing river in the expanding desert,
do you not perceive it?

Xan West is a preacher of Black Lives Matter
and other millenial liberation theologies, a
teacher of liturgical direct action, and a grass-
roots organizer that loves God. She is a Black
queer femme and a pretty darn good mom.

Facebook: Xan West

PHILIPPIANS 3:4B-14

Whitenessians: A Letter to the Church at Whitenessia

If anyone has reason to be confident in their whiteness, I have more:

confirmed white on the 8th day, well, actually it was on the 1st day, a member of the colorblind liberal tribe of the Left Coast, a white girl born among white folks; as to the law, privileged AF;

as to what is real, a perpetrator of racist ideologies; as to cluelessness about my privileged white ass under the law, not even blameless. Not. Even.

Yet whatever gains I had, these I have come to regard as loss because of whiteness.

More than that, I regard whiteness as loss because of the surpassing value it has robbed from this world, lives taken, stolen, ships full of bodies, streets running with blood, and the vacant shells that maybe, at some point in time, housed the humanity of white people. For the sake of whiteness, countless people have suffered and lost all things, and I regard whiteness as rubbish in order that I might free myself from whiteness over and over and over and over again

and to be found free, not having any righteousness of my own that comes from the law of whiteness, but one that comes from the realization that I can never fully repay or repair the damage whiteness has done and all that I have gained by just existing in my skin.

I want to know freedom and the power of a resurrection from whiteness by becoming humble, and awkward, and unafraid,

if I somehow may attain a resurrection from whiteness

Not that I have already attained this or have already reached the goal; but I press on to make it my own, because otherwise I will die. Or worse yet, I will be like the walking dead, a white zombie eating the brains of Blackness, but never ever loving the living. Whiteness creates monsters – it is a horror show.

Beloved, I do not consider that I have made it on my own out of whiteness; but this one thing I will remember always; whiteness is a lie that seeks to destroy what lies behind and steal what lies ahead,

I press on toward the goal for the prize of the heavenly resurrection from whiteness. I call in the name of a freedom that surpasses all understanding. Amen.

Jean Jeffress *holds a Master's of Divinity from American Baptist Seminary of the West in Berkeley, CA. She is a candidate for ordination in the United Church of Christ. She is a member and lay leader of First Congregational Church of Oakland, and a member of Second Acts, a liturgical direct action group in Oakland, CA.*

Twitter at @jeanj199

PHILIPPIANS 2:5-11

The Blood of the Ancestors

Jesus, like Buddha, is an idealization of human potential. I know that when I sit in a lotus position, with my back straight, my chin tucked, my eyes closed, my palms nested and my thumb-tips lightly touching, I am emulating a pose that calls forth something more than myself. When I stand in a pulpit on a Sunday morning, or sit in a hospital with a bereaved family, I know that I am not there just as myself, but as a channel through which the love of God — abundant, universal love — can flow.

Because the story of Jesus came to many Black people in the colonized West through the yoke of enslavement, I can't imagine a time when I won't associate his glowing, beatific face with the horrors visited upon my ancestors, and the residual abuse and violence done to Black people to this day.

Like many other Black ministers and ministers of color before me, I have to reinterpret Jesus and the Gospel story for my context, in light of the history of white supremacy and heteropatriarchy. This passage speaks to redemptive suffering, in which in exchange for a gruesome death on the cross, Jesus is ultimately exalted and granted dominion over all earth and heaven, such that everyone will confess his greatness.

Today in the United States, we see where this kind of thinking leads. At the highest levels of government, we have a patriarchal, sexist, racist, exceedingly wealthy cadre of men seeking the very kind of domination that is to be awarded to Jesus at the end of days. One person in particular seems intent on being always in the spotlight, whether through social media, on television, in the news, or in everyday conversations. Because Jesus is presented as an able-bodied white man, he is the perfect emblem for a culture and a system built on the values of white supremacy — winning at all cost, punishing people who aren't rich, groveling at the feet of even richer people, exploiting people's desperation, caring only for one's own interests in a very narrow way.

When I think of those who took on the nature of a servant, who humbled themselves and became obedient to death, I think of the countless Mississippians, famous and lesser-known, who tilted the arc of the moral universe toward justice. I think of Fannie Lou Hamer of Ruleville, and the abuse she sustained because she knew that her expression of her own divinity depended on affirming her humanity. She challenged the status quo through boldly seeking the right to vote. I think of Medgar Evers under his carport, attached to a house with no front door because he feared that would make him too easy a target. It didn't matter: He was still felled by the bullet of a coward in the dark who was more invested in maintaining the status quo that denied access to voting rights for Black people. Medgar had worked for years to secure those rights for himself and all the rest of us.

I lift up the story of Vernon and Ellie Dahmer (pronounced DAY-mur) of the Hattiesburg area. In this same time of wanton violence and voter suppression, the Dahmers were another bold progressive family caught in the crossfire of history. Because of their activism, they became the target of a Ku Klux Klan raid that left their house burned to the ground, and Mr. Dahmer's lungs fatally filled with smoke. He and Mrs. Dahmer exchanged fire with the attackers. While she and their children survived, he would lose his life. Their story is hardly known, and it certainly wasn't part of what I learned in Mississippi History in the late 1970s. She is yet with us today, in her 90s and a powerful witness to a terrible chapter of history.

Fannie Lou Hamer. Medgar Evers. Vernon Dahmer. These are the ones who come to mind when I consider those who made themselves nothing, who took on the nature of servants and humbled themselves, becoming obedient unto death, even by assassination, neglect, and mob violence. This is why, when I take communion, I am mostly thinking of them and their sacrifices.

These are the ones whom I seek to follow. I don't think they did what they did for the promise of glory and honor in another life. I believe they knew their obedience to love meant there would be more love and freedom in the world in time. They themselves might not receive the gifts of it, but others would. They were already bigger than those who hated them, and they knew it. They had nothing to prove about their worth and dignity. They simply refused to bow down to oppression, choosing to be their most authentic selves rather than what white supremacists would have dictated. May we, in this deeply troubled time, follow their example and live out the fullness of our values, even if that means great personal sacrifice for the good of humankind and our planet.

*Rev. **Carlton Elliott Smith** is an ordained minister in the Unitarian Universalist Association. Born and raised in Holly Springs, Mississippi, he has served as parish minister at congregations in Metro New York; Oakland, California; Greater Boston and Northern Virginia. He is currently a member of the UUA's Congregational Life Team for the Southern Region. At the time of this publication, he had just become a candidate for Mississippi State Senator representing Senate District 10, which includes Holly Springs, his place of residence since 2013.*

PHILIPPIANS 3:13-14

Press on for Justice!

The late James Cone once said: "the Gospel of liberation is bad news to all oppressors because they have defined their "freedom" in terms of slavery of others."

We have to press to a place that will eradicate thinking that puts people in a box. God made us all different. He made short, tall, heavy, light, brown, black, white and all the shades in between. The best personal liberation is when we can be okay with ourselves. In many cases we don't like ourselves and that sends us to a place where we don't like others, as well. The Bible says in Luke 6:31 "And as ye would that men should do to you, do ye also to them likewise" (KJV). The problem with this scripture is that people don't love themselves, and we wonder why they treat others in a horrible way.

The Apostle Paul is very open with us in the Scriptures. Philippians 3 identifies a few pressing desires that dominated his life. These desires are so vital that every Christian should strive to reach them in life. Although Paul is a high class Jew, free-born Roman citizen, with great prospects for the future, when he found Christ, he abandons all of what he knows and decides to get to know Him more. When Paul received a clear revelation and vision of Christ, he abandoned everything for three pressing desires.

If Paul could "press" to a more perfect way, I feel that we can as well. I want to encourage us to do the same. We have an obligation to liberate, and to press to a better day. Let us commit to fighting for justice in a way that would challenge the current system of oppression. Let us speak to an inequality that would allow wages to be the same for those working the same jobs. Let us move to a time where people can love each other without concerning themselves with who their parents are or what type of education they possess. Let us press towards a day where we can compare it to the past and say we have come a mighty long way. But the question is how do we get there?

1 - We have to have a personal knowledge of Christ. Verses 7 & 8 show us the type of salvation that Paul knew. It was a performance based salvation. This was secondhand, however Paul sought to know Christ for himself. Based off of Paul's upbringing, it is easy to say that he was a privileged individual. Paul shows us a wonderful testimony that you can actually press pass "privilege" and seek knowledge of more than what you have been exposed to. If our society would strive to expose themselves to more than themselves, we could come to know the plight of other races, sexes and social economic differences.

2 - Personal Perfection in Christ - Verses 12 and 13 show us that Paul claimed no perfection in the flesh, but he sought after perfect holiness in Christ Jesus. He had laid hold of Jesus because Jesus had laid hold of him, and Jesus was to him his all in all. Paul was in hot pursuit of Christian perfection. His conduct is not regulated nor influenced by that of others; he considers only his calling, his Master, his work, and his end. If others think they have time to loiter or trifle, he has none: time is flying; eternity is at hand; and his all is at stake. So Paul runs to obtain the prize…keeping his eyes on his lane and on his goal. So for us the same is true. What is our call, what is our fight, what is our mandate from the Kingdom? Dr. Martin Luther King Jr. said "injustice anywhere, is a threat to justice everywhere." There is injustice all around us, and we have to answer the call to fight!

3 - A Personal Possession of Christ - Verse 14 Paul presses toward the mark; the goal at the end of the course. For the prize of the high calling of God in Christ Jesus; the prize which God's heavenly calling has in view. This is what we argue about. What is in God's view?

Let us remember what we should be fighting for. There are two sides of the fight 1) those that are in the fight for change to a better way and 2) those that are in the fight to maintain the current way. Which side of the fight will you be on? Christ's message for us was to be change agents in the world. Paul made a decision that he would come to know the ways of Christ and put them into action. We cannot just know who Christ is, we have to do what Christ did. We have to push for equality, press for change, and pursue justice at any cost. This means standing up to the status quo, marching for equal work - equal pay, and screaming for a legal system that is fair regardless of race, sex, and economics.

Keep Pressing for Justice!

The Reverend Dr. **Jerret Fite** is the Pastor of New Mt. Olivet A.M.E. Zion Church in Rock Hill, SC. He is the husband of Andrea Fite and the proud father of Jeremiah, Aaron and Maya. Pastor Fite is a Graduate of North Carolina Central University with a BA in Political Science with a minor in History, Gardner-Webb University with a Masters of Divinity, and Hood Theological Seminary with a Doctorate of Ministry.

Facebook Jerret Fite
Instagram jcfite
Twitter @JerretFite

WEEK SIX

Sixth Sunday
in Lent

PSALM 118:1-2, 19-29

Anthem of Assurance

O give thanks to the Lord, for the Lord our God never quits!

How can we be grateful when there are so many uncertainties in life, frustrations that come with the human experience, that cause feelings of loneliness and confusion, that are brought on by the unpredictable behaviors of those in the Empire? Numbness caused by paralyzing thoughts of another Black or brown body lying cold in the streets. Grief that saturates and soaks the soul of a mother that has lost her baby to another senseless killing. Pain felt for the young woman that will never get to see her unborn child because her light was put out too soon....

These are the faces that have been sketched in our minds by those of the Empire. They are the many sides of a prism that society has tried to make us believe render us whole and complete.

Watch out for Stranger Danger; they warned as we left the safety of our homes to walk the streets each day!

These are they!
Strangers that have fragmented our dreams...
Trigger-happy police and unauthorized citizens that patrol our neighborhoods, through misguided systems of justice.

These are they! The danger zones...those places that have sent our psyches into places unknown.

As we try to face our new realities with the uncanny twists and turns that seem foreign to our souls and spirits, excuses, not exaltation, meet these polarized times. The temporary fixes we come up with serve as imposters for the results we need. They are polite ways of rejecting hope and they rob us and leave us bankrupt.

These are the strangers they warned us about!

The only way to harness the danger of them is to put them before a power greater than they are. The only way to bring them under submission is to place before them a force that is more sustaining than any logical thought the human mind can conceive. These strange and dangerous images must be met with a song that the soul can recognize.

A word of hope!
An anthem of assurance!
A message of certainty!
Psalm 118 says that God never quits!

When the soul is seeking refuge it can find provisions for head and heart when it knows that God never quits!

When the psyche searches for ways to be grateful, it looks for a compass. O, Give thanks to the Lord, for he is good! It is The Lord that starts with a promise and ends with the same! His staying power never quits!

His position remains steady as it weaves between the lines of our hope and despair, co-laboring in the work of justice to defend us from harm. The power of His might will bust the gates of hell wide-open to dismantle the excuses of the Empire...because God never quits!

O, give thanks to the Lord, for He is good!
His mercy endures forever!
His lovingkindness is everlasting!
God never quits!

In the midst of the dark nights, God never quits!
When cloudy days come, God never quits!
When the challenges of life become too much, His truth reigns and God never quits!

O, Give thanks to the Lord!
Not for the horror.
Not for the terror.
Not for the violence.
Not for the unresolved pain.

Not for the injustice.

Not for the Empire!

O, give thanks to The Lord, for the Lord our God illuminates us with His grace!

O, give thanks to The Lord, for the Lord our God has given us freedom!

O, give thanks to The Lord, for the Lord our God, He is God!

O, give thanks to The Lord, for the Lord our God is our salvation!

O, Give thanks to the Lord for the Lord our God never quits!

*Dr. **Carolyn Yvette Baldwin** is an ordained minister at Mt. Pleasant Baptist Church (MPBC) in Alexandria, VA. As a trained psychologist, she has developed a skill and passion for teaching others about the impacts of disabilities and trauma. She has an earned Ph.D. in Counseling and Educational Psychology w/minors in Neurological Psychology and Assessments from Loyola University as well as a M.Div. from The Samuel DeWitt Proctor School of Theology (STVU) at Virginia Union University.*

Facebook: @CarolynBaldwin

LUKE 22:14-23:56

Bitter Drink

Progressing towards what appears to be the place of our slaughter
Seeking to quench our thirst in His wondrous wells of Living water
Yearning for justice to prevail and bring forth righteousness' source
Wondering, why we are unjustly crucified daily on this hell's course
Nailed to the cross for those who seem to show no signs of remorse
Pedal to the metal, without any shame, full throttle maximum force
Crying out to God, "Why are we fated.to drink this cup of divorce?"

God's will prevails as our mission for this spin around the
world for sure
Yet we have grown weary of the stripes of distress we
continuously endure
In our likeness, we perceive residue of all our sin past,
present, and future
Adversely upon our backs, we carry the chastisement
of all men's inflictions
A study of the juxtaposition of contradictions woven into
digestible fiction
Painfully inciting friction with our basic intuition throughout
its duration
We cannot continue ingesting the delicate narration of
our domination

Inwardly our soul cries out for God to take this cup without hesitation
For examination of its content fills us with an excess of lamentations
Within the matter is the disenfranchisement of marginalized sections
Tossed to and fro, every which way imagined shaken without direction
Sick and tired of rejection and denied expectations without
ramifications

Yet some request our silence since strides have somewhat
been obtained
Though today's headlines still make us wonder what's really
been gained

As we reflect, we examine further into this rank cup for God's objectives
Knowing that all that happens to us is part of his predestinated directives
Working towards our good and ultimate purpose for his treasure creation
Nothing has happened by happenstance or without his marvelous
causation
In all history, even beyond, the original strange fruits postured upon a
holy tree
Without any sins upon his heavenly shoulders, dying to set all nations
truly free
God's will has been accomplished through the manipulation of many
structures

No matter how corrupt or bent on self-exaltation and preservation
of culture
God's will nevertheless persevere, emerging through like the
almighty Nile
Strong and true without an apparent course but far from running
truly wild
It's path and ways unknown to man but ultimately guided by
God's prowess
Thus just as Jesus suffered pain purposefully, we must allow him
to endow us
Not to endure unto death the suffering but the strength to
spiritedly pursue
For the right cessation of the supremacy of one entity is
undeniably overdue

Just as God's will actualizes itself even within the tool of opposition
at the cross
So shall justice be won through the Trojan horse in the confines
of a society lost
In these days of never-ending turmoil, we have still been able to
remain upright

Even when we have had to take a knee alone while others grew furiously uptight

However, I believe that all shall soon awaken from intoxicating sleep that binds
Eradicating from our collective sleepy eyes a soothing enchantment that blinds
Realizing that God is quite able to change the situation faster than we can blink
Thus as he partook of his cup so shall we purposefully consume this bitter drink

R. C. Ferguson *is an unconventional minister focused on faith, community upliftment, and social change, as well as an author and educator by trade. Her literary works include poetry, devotionals, children fiction, and Christian fiction. Additionally, she is a high school math teacher. Ferguson is a proud graduate of Fayetteville State University. However, the titles she esteems most are a loving wife and adoring mother.*

Facebook: R. C. Ferguson
Instagram : rcferguson716
Twitter: @RFerguson716

LUKE 19:28-40

The Gospel According to White Folks – Palm Sunday

The first thing white folks would do
is demand another gospel

for the story about honoring Jesus
and scoring a premium seat at the safer
of this week's two parades
by pulling fronds off someone else's palm trees.

It's called "Palm Sunday" for God's sake
and there isn't a palm in sight.

Luke is all about taking off our own clothes
and laying them on the ground
to be completely ruined
by donkey hooves and donkey dung.

And white folks really do not like
stripping down
so we can be seen, really seen,
and maybe we won't even get our own coat
back again at the end of the day,

and need to keep warm inside
what someone else is willing to give us.

But somewhere between
the comfortable deforestation of other gospels
and the way a too-tight collar

that chokes off any real "hosanna,"
is the unlikely miracle
of joining the ragtag choir of stones.

Maren C. Tirabassi *is white. Her most recent book is* A Child Laughs –
Prayers for Justice and Hope, *an anthology with seventy-seven writers
from eleven countries. She is a guest preacher, new author mentor, and
workshop facilitator with prison inmates, new English speakers, and cancer and dementia patients.*

blog: giftsinopenhands@wordpress.com
Facebook: Maren Tirabassi
Casa: An Experiment in Doing Church Online, RevGalsBlogPals

PSALM 31:9–16

piedmont

I had heard about the November 1979 massacre in Greensboro
but not in a way that stuck.
Like in the mud stuck. U-haul trailer hitch backed up
into Piedmont red clay embankment kind of mud stuck.
Learning of it will not let you go.

32 years later
when a survivor asks me where I am from
and I say "Rowan County,"
her eyes open up a little wider
her mouth says "that's Klan country."

part of me wants to say no. can't be.
can be, though:

> (one keg into a spring fling
> party, the college kids come gun toting
> a friend loses his teeth
> blood slings across the hood of my car
> and we herd inside and into the kitchen
> when, before cell phones, Drew
> licks his pinky & ring-finger
> and shuffles through the white pages.

"who are you calling" I ask, breath gone.
Drew stares low: "the Klan.")

"that's right," I tell her.

then it stuck.

39 years later
my kin goes to a country church where all my

people's bones are buried. a few elders don't
want the black lives matter sign
next to where the nativity scene goes in winter
where the empty robed cross stands in spring

i tell her about the murdered five,
how just down the road from church
was where Klan were recruiting months before
they gunned the five down.

so I say a compromise might be a sign that reads
"no Klan welcome here."
she shakes her head and says, "I don't know how that would go over."

and then tonight I turn a screen on
and read how the Greensboro police
hog-tied Marcus
and he died. The autopsy ruled it a homicide.

"officers followed all procedures"
"they did not violate any policies"

when they think they have finally found a way to
murder us
it will be because our memories no longer linger
on the tongues of our children.

but with hope, out where the lines
in the road are faded
and the blacktop, now gray,
has crumbled around the edges
there might be a slip into a
patch where the weeds are thin

and when they pick themselves up off
the ground and wipe the
stain into their palms,
they'll start to remember
because blood is
in the clay.

Allyn Maxfield-Steele is the Co-Executive Director of the Highlander Research & Education Center in New Market, TN. He is an ordained minister in the Christian Church (Disciples of Christ). He considers Rowan County, NC, home, although he currently lives in Haywood County, NC, with his spouse, Erin, an Episcopalian priest.

ISAIAH 50:4-9A

An Indictment

It was 2014 and the Genesis Clergy Leadership had written a short reflection entitled "Black Lives Matter" to be distributed to the 500+ people in our database. Shortly after I hit "send," I received a note from a long-time supporter of Genesis. She stated that she would stop her e-donation to Genesis unless we "retracted" the email. I was taken aback as this is a woman who is devoted to her Church, a supporter of our justice-agenda, and (I assumed) a white ally.

I took several deep breaths and composed and deleted several indignant replies. And then I remembered who I was. I have been a community organizer for more than 10 years. Before that I worked as a social worker for 12 years. These jobs call me to express love for the community, and relationships are everything.*

So I sent her one line: "Can we have lunch?"

She agreed and we met. Cut to the chase: we did not agree at the end of our lunch. She began with how much she believes in our mission of racial and economic equity. She just did not understand how the mission was connected to "Black Lives Matter."

I felt a severe moment of cognitive dissonance.... I was so disappointed that this woman, a follower of Jesus, simply DID NOT GET IT. I walked away from the meeting unsettled, but grateful that she was willing to meet and we could have our discourse.*

It was then that I felt it...an indictment.

Google defines an indictment as, "a thing that serves to illustrate that a system or situation is bad and deserves to be condemned."

I felt like I (we) in Genesis had not done a good enough job. I am a product of white supremacy and have clearly benefited from being "a model minority" as a Chinese-American woman. "Model minority," in my view, means that I "act white."

I had not lifted up race and the clear way that Black/brown people are affected. I had not demonstrated that Black Lives Matter.

Since that moment, I have committed to making sure I correct this; my resipiscence has involved the inclusion of Black/brown youth in the center of our work and direct and open conversations about race/white supremacy/white privilege in all of our meetings. None of this happens in a comfortable space. I still make mistakes, which are often my best teachers.

Also, I am committed to opening my heart to the white brothers and sisters who are trapped in a system of white supremacy. It is not enough to be indignant and walk away. We need to try our best to be part of the resipiscence of others. It is perhaps one of the best ways of loving the other.*

*even when we don't agree.

Mary Lim-Lampe is the Executive Director of Genesis, the Bay Area affiliate of the Gamaliel Network. She was called into organizing during a "perfect storm" at a Gamaliel Network organizer training when a good agitation by her mother was followed by her throwing up and making a decision to come out of the shadows and build power in community. She graduated cum laude from the University of Missouri-St. Louis (BA-Political Science) and has a juris doctorate from St. Louis University-School of Law. Mary began her work as the community organizer for MORE2 (Metro Organization for Racial and Economic Equity), the Gamaliel Affiliate in Kansas City, Missouri (her hometown). The biggest reason "why" Mary works in the justice field is her 13 year old daughter, Caitlyn.

LUKE 23: 1-49

Headline News: Unarmed Dark-Skinned Man Arrested, Beaten in Gethsemane and Lynched at The Skull

From Wire Reports – Resipiscence News

Members of the community are stunned as overnight, another unarmed dark-skinned man was arrested in Jerusalem and later lynched at the place called The Skull. Shortly after midnight, a popular local rabbi known for speaking truth to power in the City Temple and in the streets, was seized by the chief priests and elders of the synagogue for riotous teaching. According to the arrest warrant, the dark-skinned man, identified as the Son of Man with multiple aliases of Jesus, Teacher, and the Messiah, caused a commotion in the Garden of Gethsemane when the temple police came for him. Hours later, after being beaten, flogged and derided by the chief priests, the rabbi was crucified on a public hill as onlookers, including his mother, watched him take his final breath.

This comes just three days after four other unarmed dark-skinned men were arrested and severely beaten. As the community continues to be at unrest, civic leaders in the mostly Black neighborhood of Jerusalem's southern sector have taken to the streets to protest this latest killing of Black-skinned and dark brown-skinned men at the hands of the police. Bartholomew, a long-time community activist and close follower of Jesus, said he had been with the rabbi earlier in the evening at a community dinner with other close followers. "Militarized policing is alive and well in this city, and every Black-skinned and dark brown-skinned man's life is at stake. This is why we organize and galvanize for change in the system. This is why we protest in the streets and shout, 'Black Lives Matter.' They killed the Messiah and strung him up on a tree like he was a nobody. He was out here preaching the truth and pushing for change."

According to witnesses, another follower of the rabbi, Peter, was heard refuting claims that he was in fact an associate and disciple of the controversial teacher. When asked about this, Bartholomew said, "There have always been some in the struggle who will turn on you when the stakes are high." Sources close to the case say that the approximately thirty-three-year-old Jesus, with no record of prior arrests, was brought before the Governor and charged with a list of offenses, and that initially there was no basis to hold him. An attorney for Jesus' family said when the courts couldn't find a legal reason to hold him, they fabricated charges against him.

"They falsely accused him of perverting the nation, which he didn't do. They questioned his credentials as a prophet, insisting that he wasn't who he said he was. And when that didn't work, they lied and said he stirs up the people by teaching and preaching throughout all Judea, from Galilee where he began his ministry," said Theo Merritt, a civil rights attorney representing the rabbi's family. "He was lynched for speaking truth to power, for disrupting the status quo and for preaching a message of social justice. When that truth begins to dismantle these systemic structures of institutionalized racism, hegemony and patriarchy, it's like a check-mate move where the person is just some pawn that you can knock off. We will continue to protest and speak truth to power. The system can't take all of us out. We will not rest."

"It was the strangest thing," said one witness who spoke on the condition of anonymity for fear that he might be next. "Part of the crowd stood there mocking him and saying, 'If you're the King of the Jews, why don't you save yourself?' They even cast lots to see who would get his clothes. It's like killing dark-skinned people is a game to them."

In what can best be described as a chain of strange events, witnesses say that a total solar eclipse happened at noon, and that the curtain of the temple was torn in two just as Jesus took his final breath and uttered, "Father, into your hands I commend my spirit." Community leaders say plans are underway for a "Remembrance Rally" that will honor the life and work of the rabbi. They promise to keep his name alive and to continue the social justice work of Jesus' ministry. "We will not rest until the lives of every Black-skinned and dark brown-skinned body is valued just as much as the fair-skinned bodies," said Merritt.

Yvette R. Blair-Lavallais *is a Methodist elder serving in Dallas, and is a co-founder of Miles of Melanin, a non-profit that dismantles the barrier of expenses for melanated activists, writers and artists to attend liberative conferences and workshops one travel grant at a time. She is a doctoral of ministry student at Memphis Theological Seminary, a 2018 fellow of Vanderbilt Divinity School's inaugural Public Theology and Racial Justice Collaborative and she is a 2017 fellow of Princeton Theological Seminary's Black Leadership Theology Institute. She is a writing coach and editor.*

Yvetteblair.com
@YvetteRevYBlair on Twitter
IG preachergirl716

PHILIPPIANS 2:5-11

Running on Empty

"Model your minds after Christ," Paul says.

"Let God's mind be your mind," Paul says.

What human would be so confident as to believe that s/he could have the mind of Christ? What does that even look like? Paul doesn't neglect to explain it, and in doing so, the idea seems untenable. It all starts with nothing, emptying one's self of one's self and then serving. To put it plainly, running on empty.

Selfless humility is how the amplified version articulates it. Yes, it sounds redundant. Why have both selflessness and humility? Where one is found, does the other not follow? According to Paul, they are not one in the same, and Paul uses the example of Jesus to show the difference.

Jesus, who possessed the purest essence of God, emptied himself of his divine attributes to become like us, human. He emptied Himself to run down here to earth and serve us, those who are not worthy to touch a tassel on his robe. In His humanity, Jesus could have been prideful; He had every right to boast in his divinity. He is, after all, the son of God. Jesus did not flaunt His lineage but rather became a servant to man in obedience to God. In this way, Jesus was exhibiting not just selflessness but also humility. It couldn't have been easy to do.

To know that on the inside you are one who is divine in nature; to understand that you are credentialed and monied and talented and skilled beyond comprehension; to experience a divinity that cannot be articulated with words; and to still walk circumspectly, lowly, humbly, and with a heart and hand of servitude among men and women takes a special sort of emptying, the type of emptying that we cannot imitate easily.

Empty: You are not reaching back for stored up stock dividends or money market accounts, network opportunities or terminal degrees, credentials or titles. You have emptied yourself of dependence on such things. You are an obedient servant who reaches up for instructions from God. You pull His purpose down into your bosom. You extend your hands in servitude toward a world full of injustice, inequality, oppression, denigration, poverty, biases, and setups, with your palms full of the purpose God has given for that day. You serve. You are emptied again. You pray for bread the next day. You repeat.

This is the mind of emptiness. This is the mind of Christ. Christ emptied Himself of Himself so much that there was nothing inside of Him but the will of His Father. He had no other mind than the mind of service, the mind of obedience, a mind and body that served us here on earth even unto death. Likewise, the life of servitude does not require that I sacrifice some things, rather, true servitude requires me to empty myself of everything as the will of God requires. My best service is offered when I am completely empty. My best worship occurs when I empty myself of everything as a living sacrifice to God. God's best, Jesus Christ, emptied himself so much that at His name every single knee will be coaxed to bend.

Empty = Exalted. It makes no sense, especially in this day and age. The more we fill our pages and tweets and grams and snaps with likes and hearts and thumbs up, the more exalted we become. It's the way of the world: fill up and feel good. I even exalt my car over all other cars when it's full of gas. On empty, my car is of no use to me. I am, we are, programmed for full. Even in servitude, we want full participation, full exposure, full recognition, full credit. The more people we can get to see us serving, the better we feel. The selflessness may seem apparent, but the humility is lacking—maybe even false. But it is not like that for believers. This is not the true mind of Christ; it is a sullied image of what we want people to believe is Christ in us.

Selfless humility must be our true intent in our service to others, or else at the bottom of all the serving, we may find that we are serving ourselves and essentially full of ourselves. I want to look like Christ. I want His mind to be my mind—His attitude, mine. I acknowledge fully that means pouring out the parts of myself that don't look like Him. It's hard to do. But if I couldn't do it, God wouldn't ask it of me. Selfless humility: the best path to true servitude, so empty yourself and run.

DiAnne Malone *is Vice President of Student Affairs at the Memphis Center for Urban Theological Studies in Memphis, TN. She also teaches African and African American Studies at the University of Memphis. She has published nonfiction work in literary journals, self-published a 40-day devotional, and edited an anthology of essays. Along with her colleague, she has written several novellas in a series called, The Church Chronicles of Iris and Locke.*

Facebook @ DiAnne Malone
Twitter @AphroDiAnne
Website https://www.diannemalone.com

WEEK SEVEN

Holy Week

PSALM 70

Psalm of a Tired Black Woman

For the chanters. Of color. A proffering.

1   El Shaddai!!!!!!! Please rescue me from the bigots of this world and their oppressive systems.

> Come quickly to my side for my hands are up, I cannot breathe, and I didn't kill myself.

2   May those who treat me like my black life does not matter

> Be shamed in person and on the interwebs, fired, discredited, and removed from power.

May those who take pleasure in harmful hoarding of resources and dehumanizing policies

> Be denied their great America bootstrapped lie.

3   May those who say "All Lives Matter", "Blood and Soil", "You Will Not Replace Us", "Make America Great Again", "I Don't See Color", "What Happened Before The Video?", "They Should Have Complied", "There Is No Such Thing As White Supremacy," "Playing The Race Card"

> Be withdrawn, reflect, and experience resipiscence.

4   But, may seekers of Love

> Intone and protest and celebrate and breathe with intention.

Let all those who adore you and appreciate the way you value relationship
> Say, "Elohim is great!"

5   But as for me, I am weary and poured out, steadily losing my song and smile and sleep.

Draw near now, Shammah, without delay, yesterday.

You are my liberator and bearer of justice

Sabaoth, do not tarry. Do not deny. No longer can I (we) wait.

Vahisha Hasan is a faith-rooted organizer working at the intersections of faith, social justice, and mental health. She is an Assistant Professor of Human Services at Memphis Center for Urban and Theological Studies (MCUTS) and the Executive Director of Movement in Faith, a project of Transform Network. She is a powerful public speaker, transformative facilitator, social justice trainer, minister, and writer with a deeply prophetic voice and imagination for how faith communities can be an active part of collective liberation. She co-edited Resipiscence 2018 and 2019 with Nichola Torbett and is grateful for every contributor and reader that yearns for a better expression of faith and more depth in our demand for justice.

Facebook: @MovementInFaith
Twitter: @VHasanMIF
Instagram: vhasanlifebetter
Websites: https://www.transformnetwork.org/vahisha-hasan
            https://www.transformnetwork.org/mif-projects/
Email: movementinfaith@gmail.com

1 CORINTHIANS 11: 23-26

Memories and Tables

Anyone who has taken communion has probably heard this passage from 1 Corinthians 11 enough times to recite it from memory. Since my church experience has been ecumenical, I have taken communion in numerous ways--from kneeling before an altar to receiving a communion "snack pack." More often than not, I have focused on ensuring that my hands were positioned correctly or my skirt didn't rise while kneeling, or that I properly removed the plastic from the "snack pack." Paul's words, though familiar, have been background noise to the trappings of the communion ritual. I decided it was necessary to read I Corinthians 11 as if doing so for the very first time.

My fresh reading provided new insights about the passage which connect with my unapologetically Black and Christian heritage: memories and the table. Put simply, we come to the table to remember. Whether it is the table of the Lord's Supper or Grandma's dinner table, the table has been and continues to be a part of the collective memory of Christians and African Americans.

When I was growing up, my family ate together most evenings. One of my fondest memories around the dinner table is our parents reciting poetry from the likes of Paul Lawrence Dunbar and Margaret Walker. This ritual was my parents' way of keeping us connected to our cultural roots in a changing 1970s world. Both my parents worked in the Greensboro Movement, desiring a world in which their children didn't experience racial segregation, oppression and terror. Yet they wanted us to remember that struggle. Through Black poetry around the dinner table, we remembered.

One poem I heard recited many times during those family dinner moments was Langston Hughes' "I, Too." It reads:

I too sing America
I am the darker brother
They send me in the kitchen when company comes, but I laugh
and eat well
and grow strong.

Tomorrow, I'll be at the table when company comes.
Nobody'll dare say to me, "Eat in the kitchen," then.
Besides, they'll see how beautiful I am and be ashamed
I, too, am America.

Recently, after one of many police brutality cases hit the news, my 30-year-old sister posted Hughes's poem on Facebook. I was distressed by my sister's need to affirm, fight even, for her place at America's table, just as our father and grandparents had done, so she wouldn't have to. Why do people who have fought and died in every war on this soil and throughout the world, a group that believed enough in this country's foundational documents to urge it "to live out the true meaning of its creed," still have to cry, "Hey, me too! I belong here. I matter"? In my distress, I read "I, Too" anew.

While the timelessness of Hughes' poem is lamentable, I am drawn into his metaphor of the table. I have tended to focus solely on Hughes's opening line about being sent to the kitchen, and his transitional line "tomorrow, I'll be at the table when company comes." The movement of position when company comes ring of "but God" moments where weeping brings joy. So focused have I been on "tomorrow" that I skipped Hughes' declaration about what happened in the meantime.

In the kitchen Hughes says, "But, I laugh, eat well and grow strong." Yes, while excluded from the table of the American Dream, not only did he eat, he ate well, and grew strong, and even laughed while doing so.

African American culture, rich with humor from family stories, folk-tales, and re-storied biblical texts, has evolved around the kitchen table. Rich foods and even hairstyles produced by pressing combs on hot stoves were developed at the kitchen table. The strength to face struggles through the many prayers lifted and stories told has been mustered around the kitchen table. African-American educational, cultural and religious institutions grew from our exilic "kitchen table" experience in America.

The very mechanism intended to destroy us has made us strong. At the table, we have been able to "taste and see that the Lord is good." Paul's words invite us to God's table anew, and while there we remember the table set for us by our ancestors.

Kathryn V. Stanley *is an Atlanta-based writer, editor, educator, and public theologian whose gifts support the work of Christian publishers, including Judson Press, ministers, congregations, and nonprofit organizations throughout the United States. Stanley holds degrees from Spelman College, the University of Virginia School of Law, and Emory's Candler School of Theology. Stanley chairs the women's ministry at Ebenezer Baptist Church and teaches middle school English through the lens of the social gospel.*

JOHN 13: 1-17

Maundy Thursday Realized

On that day
when their salvation was at hand,
they gathered together.
Wealthy CEOs knelt before their assembly-line workers
abandoning smart phones for towels,
and white folks took the feet of
Asian immigrants from the nail salon
and cleaning women and childcare workers
tenderly
in their hands, cupping the heels.

And we wanted nothing other than to hold one another
and eat good food that we
grew and cooked together.

On that day,
people everywhere moved their bodies
for joy
rather than penance, and
all people could dance.
Women ran admiring hands over dimpled flesh
and smiled into the mirror, and
cosmetic surgeons' offices were shuttered.

On that day, bodies ceased to be shameful,
stopped being something other people had,
something to be avoided or ignored

Or shot down.

Or incarcerated, neutralized.

Something surplus, or dangerous.

Bodies were revered,
for their many colors,
differing abilities and shapes,
scents—
miracles of incarnation,
the only way we have
on this earth
of knowing one another.

Nichola Torbett *is a spiritual seeker, recovering addict, gospel preacher, podcaster, writer, resistance fomenter, dog-walker, nonviolent direct action trainer, and aspiring race traitor. Driven by her passion for both spiritual formation and social change, she co-founded* Seminary of the Street, *a training academy for love warriors, in 2009 and* Second Acts, *a liturgical direct action affinity group, in 2014. She is co-editor of* Resipiscence: a Lenten Devotional for Dismantling White Supremacy *and a contributor to* The Word Is Resistance, *a podcast from SURJ-Faith and SURJ-Action, as well as to* Jesus Radicals, The Yoke, *and other radical discipleship publications. She likes to lock herself to things at strategic moments.*

Facebook: Nichola Torbett
Blog: https://thelongingisthecompass.wordpress.com

LUKE 23:1-49

Same Fear

Though I do not observe Lent, but Passover, as a follower of Yahshua, I have deep respect for the Gospel narratives. Growing up, one of the few Bible characters whose Blackness was acknowledged was Simon of Cyrene. While discussing toxic masculinity in the Black community with friends, I remembered The History Channel's miniseries *The Bible*. In this miniseries, the only two Biblical characters that were depicted as Black were Sampson and Satan himself (who looked like former President Barack Obama). Sampson was sexually undisciplined and at times violent--stereotypes wrongly placed on Black men. Satan is known for deceit, dishonesty and evil, additional stereotypes that have been wrongly placed on Black men. Now, after 6-years of research into the Blackness of the original peoples of Israel, I do believe Sampson would be categorized as Black today. My issue is "Why whitewash all the Bible characters in a widely publicized miniseries but depict Satan and Sampson as Black?" Why in our Sunday schools, Jesus films, etc. do we depict all characters as white until we get to Simon of Cyrene, who is made by law enforcement to help Yahshua carry the cross? Is it because, as someone made to serve, Simon of Cyrene makes us comfortable, whereas depicting Yahshua as the Black Messiah he was makes us fearful? In August 1967, J. Edgar Hoover, former head of the FBI, started the COINTELPRO program to "Prevent the rise of a 'messiah' who could unify and electrify the militant black nationalist movement."[1] Hoover's fear was Rome's fear.

Now, you may not believe in a literal interpretation of the Bible. You may not believe Abraham and Sarah literally existed, but you have to acknowledge that scribes did exist, and they wrote scripture, and these scribes did come from a non-white culture. As the scribes wrote scripture, they had in mind how these characters would have looked. Also, we cannot, after over 500 years of white Biblical depictions, ignore the color of Biblical characters under the guise of "oh well, I don't believe Abraham literally existed." To undo white supremacy, we must correct the whitewashing of the Bible, Christianity and even Judaism.

Let's examine in its full humanity the life of Simon of Cyrene. Cyrene is a country on the North coast of Africa that played a crucial role in early Christian history and served as a haven for Jews fleeing trouble in Israel.[2] Many of us do not know that Simon's partnership with Yahshua did not end with helping him bear the cross. *The New Commentary on the Whole Bible*, edited by J.D. Douglas and Philip W. Comfort, brings up the interesting possibility that Simeon called Niger who appears in Acts 13:1 is the same person as Simon of Cyrene mentioned in the Synoptic Gospels as the man who helped Jesus carry his cross.[3] We should note that Simeon is a Jewish name, and Niger is Latin for "black," so Simeon aka Simon was an African Jewish man. A further examination of the Greek and Hebrew meanings of the name Simon gives more clues to the African heritage of this character in the gospels. "Simon is a common name, from Hebrew שִׁמְעוֹן Šim'ôn, meaning "listen." It is also a classical Greek name, deriving from an adjective meaning "flat-nosed."[4] Many sub-Saharan African people have noses that have been classified as "flat-noses." (This has been used in a derogatory way, but in my opinion, this is just a physical characteristic such as being tall or short or blond or brunette). Thomas Oden even goes as far as to say the Apostle Mark and Simon of Cyrene may actually be related as Levite Jews.[5] We read in Acts 11:19-21 about the men from Cyrene and Cyprus who founded the church in Antioch. The Apostle Mark who is known as the Apostle to Africa mentions Simon with his sons Alexander and Rufus, who became prominent members of the early church; it was the Cyrenians who carried the Gospel to Greece.[6] It appears that though helping Yahshua bear the cross was one moment in a momentous day, this had a lasting impact on Simon's life and ministry. This Black hero of the Bible was changed by helping Yahshua bear the cross. This reminds me that as I walk with oppressed people, it is I, not they, who is greatly transformed. Black men and women are not new to the faith, and the witness of Simon of Cyrene proves this. If you want to end white supremacy this Lent, start by undoing the whitewashing of the Bible. Remember Ethiopia and Sudan (Nubia) were Christian countries hundreds of years before England and Germany.

1. The King Institute FBI https://kinginstitute.stanford.edu/encyclopedia/federal-bureau-investigation-fbi
2. Oden, Thomas C. "The African Memory of Mark: Reassessing Early Church Tradition." IVP Academic, 2011, pp.10.
3. Douglas, J. D. and Comfort, Philip W. "New Commentary on the Whole Bible: New Testament." Tyndale House Pub, 1990, pp.112.
4. Σἰμων. Liddell, Henry George and Scott, Robert; A Greek–English Lexicon at the Perseus Project. Perseus Digital Library, Tufts University, http://www.perseus.tufts.edu/hopper/resolveform?redirect=true.
5. Oden, Thomas C. "The African Memory of Mark: Reassessing Early Church Tradition." IVP Academic, 2011,pp.10.
6. Oden, Thomas C. "The African Memory of Mark: Reassessing Early Church Tradition." IVP Academic, 2011,pp.20

Onleilove Chika Alston *is a faith-based community organizer, speaker and writer. In 2014, she founded Prophetic Whirlwind: Uncovering the Black Biblical Destiny, a teaching ministry which bloomed into a book. She ministers often in West Africa and is passionate about connecting Hebrew communities in Africa with the diaspora for greater Biblical understanding. A native New Yorker and former foster child, she knows the gospel is truly good news to the oppressed.*

PropheticWhirlwind.com.
Twitter @PropheticWhirl
Instagram @PropheticWhirlwind
Facebook.com/PropheticWhirlwind

ISAIAH 55:1-9

Thinking While Thirsty

This passage is an invitation to abundant life.

"Run, walk, keep moving – You can do it!" These are the words repeated constantly during my workout. A morning workout to prepare physically and mentally for another day of tension and fear of what might happen today. Will another Black or Brown person fall victim to a white person whose fear results in detainment, arrest, or even death? Will another elected or appointed official decide the health and wealth of their family is threatened when those who they deem "less than" are afforded basic human rights? I then need an evening workout to clear my mind, as much as possible, and rest from the realization that many of my fears have become real – again!

Run, walk, keep moving – YOU GOT THIS!

As I continue moving, I thirst. As I continue moving, I think. As I continue moving, I am thinking while I am thirsty. I am thinking, "I am being pushed beyond my comfort zone to places I have never been and experiencing things I have never experienced before."

This moving outside, doing something new or different or challenging can quickly move you from a place of familiarity to a place of unfamiliarity, discomfort and fear. The fear of the unknown can lead us to experience a paralyzing fear of lack. Lack of security. Lack of wholeness.

In the text, the prophetic message is directed to the elite of Judah who had been exiled for over two generations, meaning the audience of this message were the children and grandchildren of those forcibly removed from their promised land, to a new foreign land after the fall of Jerusalem. Today those children and grandchildren would be called DREAMERS. The target audience for the prophet's litany of abundance are those who are not natives. Today, these people are identified as immigrants, undocumented aliens, outsiders! Alongside the context of their citizenship, gender and race, they are invited to think while thirsty. Thinking of both the good things of God's creation such as material food and water, but also beyond natural human thoughts and thirst for God, even as they examine their socio-economic status, race or gender.

The invitation to a life of abundance is extended to "everyone who thirsts." Those who are hungry and thirsty are invited to come, drink and eat. The invitation is also extended to those whose thirst is the result of their choice to spend their financial, mental, emotional and spiritual capital on what some would consider the "wrong thing." They too are invited to come, eat and delight. No matter the circumstances leading to the state of thirst, the Good News is that God invites us all to feast – FREE OF CHARGE.

Racism and white supremacy fear the litany of abundance. Why? Because there is no restriction on the promised abundance. Abundance does not serve the capitalistic narrative of scarcity. If we incline our ear and accept the invitation, we will find out God is not stingy. The promised banquet is not from a fast food restaurant because God does not cut corners. There is no drive through window at a banquet. No prepackaged meals at a feast. God is generous. God promises to meet not only our immediate need, but our future needs. God offers an abundance beyond our imagination and thoughts. Despite how it appears, God offers to refresh our soul. God offers to strengthen our hearts. God promises us repeatedly that yielding to God allows the world to witness our empowerment and allows us to live into our promised identity--an identity of wholeness, an identity of security, an identity of life more abundantly. God extends an invitation to us to taste the joy of quenched thirst, of hunger gratified, and of our deepest longing satisfied.

Run, walk, keep moving – YOU GOT THIS!

> God, move me out of my comfort zone and allow me to thirst for what you have for me amid fear. I praise you because your ways are higher than my ways. Help me to be humble so that I am open to your leading. Show me the places that you are using my discomfort to draw me closer to you. I pray your kingdom would come and your will would be done in me and through me in my everyday life—on earth as it is in heaven. In the name of the Black Messiah, Jesus, I pray. Amen

Regina D. Clarke *has Masters degrees in Divinity and Christian Education with an emphasis in Ethics and Social/Restorative Justice from Samuel Dewitt Proctor School of Theology. She has a heart burst for the Deaf, the Hard of Hearing, the abused, and those who are "forgotten or discarded" by mainstream society. Her thirst for connecting the community and the church has led her to serve in prisons, domestic violence shelters, and the community-at-large to ensure no person -- despite their past, abilities, or status -- would be denied the opportunity to learn about Jesus and walk faithfully with their God. She currently serves on the ministerial staff of Abyssinian Missionary Baptist Church in Memphis.*

PSALM 31:1-5 AND LAMENTATIONS 3:19-24

Deafening Silence

November 30, 2018

Dear Dana,

At the time of this writing, it has been 1 year, 4 months, 23 days, 0 hours, 14 minutes and 42, 43, 44 seconds since I entered into a Holy Saturday with you in remembrance. The last time I saw you alive. Breathing. Moving. I write this letter to you because it is necessary and quite cathartic. No, I am not going to out you but just want to update you since you left this plane. So much has happened that has caused my hope in humanity to wane. It cries from the smallest corner of my soul, "I'm still here." This note is penned on the eve of Advent hope with the hope of Holy Saturday in mind.

Holy Saturday is that quiet time after Good Friday and before resurrection. It's that time of "what I'm gon' do? How I'm gonna make it? Where I'm gon' get help from?" There have been small victories such as LaQuan McDonald's murderer has been convicted and lightly sentenced, churches are becoming more aware of the difference between social justice work and social charity work, operating in both realms, and Flint's water situation is somewhat better since you've last known. Yet, First Nation women are being trafficked along Lake Superior, trans women are being slaughtered by the hundreds, immigrants are being tear gassed at the border, Puerto Rico is taken advantage of and women of color, and Black women in particular, are yet victims of intimate partner violence with people saying "Don't look at it that way." Negate the cause of the situation the woman is in and celebrate her life. *Dr. Tamara O'Neal, I speak your name*

Oh the deafening silence that Holy Saturday brings! Your volume is loud! It's painful and numbing. How should I put my trust in the possibility of tomorrow? My rock and fortress lies in the grave, in this moment, with you. Who shall guide me now? Is there a cry in the wilderness for relief? Who shall incline their ear to hear the requests of the people in the margins? What is for the morrow? When will the morrow come? When will Holy Saturday's silence not consume for fear of a compassionless nation that drinks the liquor of white supremacy without ceasing and revels in male dominance? These are the things that are renewed, relieved, and supported. Great is the faithfulness of those who support and stand for it by margins of at least 53%. Yet, in the movement of time--45, 46, 47 seconds--my hope sits in the corner of my soul, wounded, and worn, crying with a faint voice, "I am still here."

Your Undaunted Widow

*Minister **Antonia Coleman** is a published poet, a Masters of Divinity student at McCormick Theological Seminary and uniquely and unapologetically a woman of God. His Daughter; Her Heart Beat. Undaunted. Antonia resides at the intersections of faith, womanism, eco-justice, and sexology. She is passionate about building healthy families; empowerment of people, and specifically women; and community sustainability. She is a member of First Church of Deliverance in Chicago.*

Instagram: theundauntedwidow
Twitter: @MsToniView
FB: https://www.facebook.com/MsToniBeTru2U/

1 PETER 4:1-8

Holy Saturday

Holy Saturday, in many traditions, is one of the forgotten days in the social calendar of Christ—coined the social calendar because, like many high holy days, Easter has been hijacked by commercialism and capitalism, and Holy Saturday just is not palatable in a privileged Christian society. Holy Saturday is the forgotten holy day for many. It has been replaced with practices for the Easter play, shopping for the last minute Resurrection Sunday garb, preparing our sanctuaries and outdoor areas for the annual Easter egg hunt.... Or we are recovering on this day from the wonderful marathon preaching at the Seven Last Words service on Good Friday. Yet, THIS is the day that speaks to the true pain of those who loved Jesus. For many unattuned preachers, they rush to the THIRD DAY, without understanding that without the death, without the mourning and reflection of Holy Saturday, there is no salvation.

Holy Saturday follows on a horrific six-hour lynching just five days after he was praised and greeted with "Hosannah!" Some of the same ones who praised him, whom he fed, walked with and talked with, would rather have a known and convicted rapist and murderer set free than to have to justify a man who stood up against the current governmental oppression. It is often easier for some to side with the known enemy than to take a risk with the innocent fighting for justice. One of many lessons we learn from this story is that it cost Jesus something to take this stand, that the fight for freedom is not free.

It was women who stood there with Jesus as he took his last breath, who didn't abandon him, who watched his lifeless body taken down from the cross. He was taken to a grave and people who loved, hated, and betrayed the Christ stood in awe and grief. Using divine imagination, feel the stillness in the air, the thickness, the tension of the next day. The twelve were nowhere to be found, hiding in fear for their lives, pretending to lose all knowledge of the preparation and hope Jesus gave them. His most intimate friends, outside of the women (marginalized in society), abandoned him, fearful of the real possibility that, if caught, they would endure an even more gruesome public death than that of their beloved Jesus.

Why do we as Christians in 2019, still not take a moment to pause and acknowledge this critical day? We ensure the busyness of our lives so that we can avoid acknowledging the real deafening silence that was experienced on that day. Is it because we are afraid of the silence? Is it because of what we may discover about ourselves in this silence? Is it because of the unabated truth that speaks in silence?

In today's world, silence often becomes submission. As long as our lane of oppression is untouched, we silence our voices instead of advocating in the areas where we hold privilege.

One of the ways to end oppression is for those that are privileged to "give up" or "sacrifice" their privilege in order to give way to the oppressed. A part of that giving up is often giving voice. As a cis man, do you give voice when sexism appears? As a heterosexual identified person, do you give voice when heterosexism appears? As an educated woman, do you give voice to the under-resourced and uneducated? Are we completely satisfied walking in our privilege because "why rock the boat?" or "it doesn't take all that?" It is easier to identify with your oppressed areas, but how often do you examine your privileged areas and give voice to those oppressed in that moment?

Jesus' death and the subsequent grieving on Holy Saturday should move us to take a moment's pause to acknowledge a mother that watched her son murdered by the police. This day is a moment to acknowledge the injustices that exist and are even more pervasive with a racist, sexist, dictator occupying the White House. This is also our time to reflect on the times when we ran, when we hid, when we intentionally turned our backs on and turned our eyes and ears away from the cries of our oppressed sisters and brothers. The time is a call to be sober, pray, and repent and acknowledge that the THIRD DAY is more than a showcase of performative redemption.

Born and raised on the Southside of Chicago, this minister believes in putting boots to the ground. Min **Tennille Power** has been active in the anti violence movement for over 20 years. She identifies as a womanist and is driven by her passion in counseling and education. She is a certified trauma informed yoga instructor, a therapist and an educator, and in her spare time she raises her three sons to make a difference in the world.

ABOUT THE EDITORS

Vahisha Hasan is a faith-rooted organizer working at the intersections of faith, social justice, and mental health. She is the Executive Director of Movement in Faith and co-founder of *miles of melanin*, a travel fund for social justice artists and activists of color. She is a powerful public speaker, transformative facilitator, writer, minister, and social justice trainer, with a deeply prophetic voice and imagination for how faith communities can be an active part of collective liberation.

She is Assistant Professor of Human Services at Memphis Center for Urban and Theological Studies (MCUTS) and serves as Director of the Mental Health Advocacy which seeks to destigmatize mental health in faith communities. She is also writing the curriculum for the addition of a bachelor's degree program in Applied Psychology.

Vahisha holds a dual Master's of Divinity and Master's of Mental Health Counseling with an Education Specialist Certification from Gardner-Webb University and a bachelor's degree in Communications with a concentration in Interpersonal Organization from The University of North Carolina at Chapel Hill.

Facebook: Vahisha Hasan, @MovementInFaith, @milesofmelanin
Twitter: @VHasanMIF
Instagram: vhasanlifebetter
Website: https://transformnetwork.org/mif-projects

Nichola Torbett is a spiritual seeker, recovering addict, gospel preacher, podcaster, writer, resistance fomenter, dog-walker, nonviolent direct action trainer, and aspiring race traitor. Driven by her passion for both spiritual formation and social change, she co-founded Seminary of the Street, a training academy for love warriors, in 2009 and Second Acts, a liturgical direct action affinity group, in 2014. She is co-editor of *Resipiscence: a Lenten Devotional for Dismantling White Supremacy* and a contributor to The Word Is Resistance, a podcast from SURJ-Faith and SURJ-Action, as well as to Jesus Radicals, The Yoke, and other radical discipleship publications. She likes to lock herself to things at strategic moments.

Facebook: Nichola Torbett
Blog: https://thelongingisthecompass.wordpress.com

ABOUT THE COVER ARTIST

Born and raised in North Carolina, Heather Tolbert (BS Emmanuel College and MS Florida Gulf Coast University) suffered both social and personal traumas as a child.

"I grew up in an all-white county; racism, discrimination, and oppression were daily realities. Due to the color of our skin, my family and I were targets for cruel treatment, including from the Ku Klux Klan. If racism was not in the school system, it was on the ball fields, and at my parent's jobs; racism was there when we went grocery shopping or if we were traveling down the road. My experience with racism has left me with a lot of emotional scars."

In addition, Heather fell victim to childhood sexual abuse by a member of the extended family and addiction and infidelity in the immediate family.

"My mother would kick out my father, who struggled with addiction, one week and accept him back the next. Or my mother would move out one week and come back the next. In trying to live above the stereotypes of white people, my parents neglected to educate us on our own culture."

Heather leaned toward visual arts and creative writing after an incident in high school: after being singled out by her teacher because of the color of her skin, Heather was physically picked up out of her desk by a white male officer, thrown to the ground, and handcuffed. This incident resulted in three warrants for Heather's arrest. A year later handcuffs were placed on Heather once again as the officer escorted her out of her English class to jail.

"I needed an outlet for my anger and every other emotion that was hard for me to express. Because I never felt like I had a voice, I never learned how to express myself verbally without getting angry and stuttering, talking too fast, or resorting to foul language. Sometimes I just burst out in tears in frustration. I started to use visual art and creative writing to help express all the things I held inside.

"I always thought that to help others or to help myself I had to speak up verbally, that that was the only way to be heard. I was wrong. My art is my voice and my art, although visual, speaks volumes, and it helps me find my voice to speak. I always try to paint with the purpose of evoking conversations."

Melanin Pride/Unity is one of a growing collection of cards that can be used as art, greeting cards, postcards, or creative ways to educate, celebrate, and unite others through Black culture/history.

"In my healing journey and as part of my goal to educate others through my art, I challenge myself to live in my Blackness and navigate what it means to me. I also challenge myself to learn about Black history and feel empowered and proud of my history and then to continue in the same fight toward liberation and equality. Without addressing my own shame, division, and discord, my hunger for pride, unity, and solidarity would not exist. I want to challenge others to wake this part of themselves up and watch the magic happen."

Altar for an action in support of the **#Frisco5**, five community members who went on hunger strike from April 21-May 7, 2016, in front of the San Francisco Police Department Mission Station to demonstrate against episodes of police brutality, use-of-force violations, and racial profiling, specifically the deaths of Alex Nieto, Mario Woods, Amilcar Perez Lopez and Luis Gongora.

*The altar was created by **Carol Robison** and **Vanessa Riles**. Carol and Vanessa are both deacons and serve on the Worship & the Arts Team at First Congregational Church of Oakland. They are also members of Second Acts, a Christian direct action affinity group.*